CW01594680

CARROL
ROWE

AN AUTOBIOGRAPHICAL NOVEL

SURVIVOR

BY CARROL ROWE

INTRODUCTION

It is only through the Divine intervention of the Holy Spirit that the contents of these pages have come into being. The Lord has effected many miracles in my life, and I hope that the reader will be enlightened to go from strength to strength within the vernacular of courage through trust and unswerving faith in the Lord and His Divine promises.

I have been through some tough times; finding it harder to explain in ordinary words, may even have added to the welter of problematic situations. Consequently, as I put my pen to paper, my only resolve is to confer profound gratitude to the powers that be, for providing that bastion of support we all need in times of crisis.

I hope something within the confines of this autobiographical novel, will serve to inspire a clearer way forward. i.e. a way that leads to deliverance. My prayers are with you the reader. May the Lord richly bless you as you touch base with each page –*Amen!*

FOREWORD

This is the first in a series of published works under the auspices of my own creative writing company CDR. I pray this book will inspire revelation and deep conviction to those who are blind to the type of moral questions tied-up with day-to-day situations we often take for granted.

I am convinced that true life factors emerging from the pages of my book, will give insight into ways forward in our quest to effect positive change, especially in the light of any type of confusion you may face.

Finally, it is an honour and a joy for me to recommend this book to you the reader. Moreover, I trust that in the wake of your own journey, you will find hope, consolation, intrigue and even laughter which will lead you to freedom.

ACKNOWLEDGEMENT

I would like to give special thanks to God, the Creator who has conferred upon me the strength and ability to write this book. Commendations also to my two younger children who have been my rock though only 12 and 9 years old. Also to my two older daughters who are part of this journey, because they were born into this equation. In similar vein, I would like to take time out to thank Lilieth Wade the Founder of Grief Matters, an Author and Grief Recovery Specialist who took time out of her busy schedule to fine tune this novel. Also Pitman Browne for proof-reading the Manuscript: For his willingness albeit patience throughout the tenure of a journey God knows he may even have found hard to fathom? His dedication, commitment and selflessness turning out to be no less than a great inspiration!

I have never had anyone believing in me and willing me on to achieving this highest goal -*that of writing my first book*! In terms of actual achievement, this has been a milestone for me, hence a big thank you again Pitman! In this life, you will always be in my spirit.

In train, let me also thank Chrispel Media for building a fashionable, elegant and eye-catching website which is now part and parcel of the promotional package.

Also my friend Pauline Watters who was a pillar of strength through some of the most difficult times of my life; For her tireless efforts in helping to put it all on to paper. I am sure that accounts within my pages will strike a familiar note with those enduring circumstances they would find perhaps too hard to print. Somewhere in all of this, I want to be encouraged in the sense that these experiences will prove a blessing in the end!

DEDICATION

To all women in society who have been affected by Domestic Violence and have survived. Also, for those sisters and brothers who are struggling to overcome. I am pleased to dedicate this book to you in order to encourage, strengthen, empower, motivate and help you rise to another level. The level that will not only change your lives but the world you live in.

Whilst journeying through different stages of my manuscript, I had to come to terms with certain types of struggles faced by women within a male dominated society. Physical, psychological, emotional and mental abuse may well have destroyed me, had it not been for the grace of God. At the end of the day, it is this wonderful grace that has been carrying me through those difficult years.

In my quest to broaden the spectrum attributed to domestic violence, I am not refraining from identifying with the male counterpart since they too have been on the receiving end as documentary evidence suggests. Let us hope that certain sisters will be inclined to take stock of repercussions arising from physical, emotional and psychological abuse levelled against some of our men.

Domestic violence affects every culture, class and status in life; **remember, you are never too young or old, rich or poor to experience an assault on your own dignity and right to individual freedom.**

May my book bring to all who read through its pages, hope and renewed inspiration in the face of one woman's courage to overcome the forces of domestic violence, school bullying and other related issues.

SURVIVOR

First published in 2014
by CDR Writing and Production Ltd

For further enquiries in relation to the contents of these pages,
either go to www.carrolrowe.com

or make contact through this email address:
info@carrolrowe.com
Mob: 07832863137

Printed by Heron Press UK Partnership
59 The Avenue, Rubery Industrial Estate
Rubery, Birmingham B45 9AL
T: 0121 4574810
F: 0121 4574812
W: www.heronpress.co.uk

Book Cover: Designed by Chrispel Media
Email:info@chrispelmedia.com

Proofreading and layout by Pitman Browne

ISBN 978-0-9531493-7-7

REVIEWS

In terms of a review of Carrol's autobiographical novel, I am convinced there must have been times when she cried whilst putting some of these chapters together.

On reflection, I can remember children who were the subject of strict parenting, border-lining some of the situations you have expressed.

She is a strong character to be able to withstand hardships and setbacks, yet coming through the hurdles to a fine finish!

Councillor Merlita Bryan

Carrol provides an intimate diary of a hard life being brought up as part of the Jamaican community. Without self-pity she describes bullying and hardship from three angles; but she also describes support and help she received from brothers and neighbours.

The narrative gives an insight into a story which is rarely told.

Councillor Graham Chapman

Survivor by Jamaican born, Nottingham based author, Carrol Rowe, is the extraordinary first novel written joining the developing genre of modern Black British, autobiographical literature. The novel aims to enlighten and to explore the personal experiences of a young Jamaican girl now woman living in the UK.

Without the inclusion of the narrator's name, the story charts the harrowing and brutal life experiences of the narrator, encapsulated within a destructive world of domestic violence, largely induced by her violent father, school bullies and a deceitful first love, called Roger.

The novel, written in first- person and littered with vivid description and beautifully written prose, is interjected with phrases in upper case to scream a point at times, adding to the narrator's desire to be heard and heard clearly. The author gives a very personal, intimate and yet disturbing picture of how she became the woman of courage and strength that she is today. The style is reminiscent of black feminist theological writings in that the nature (and gender) of God is questioned and woman's relationship with nature and other women, is fundamental in finding a way forward through resilience, independence and leading to survival and a life of one's own.

Survivor is the first of many books to be published by the author, in a similar way to the autobiographical, publishing feats of the great African American writer, Dr Maya Angelou. An excellent novel and well worth a read!

Norma Gregory: *Writer/Journalist/Educator*
Majotu Magazine/ Nottingham News Centre

A must read as this inspiring autobiography forces you to think about life and empowers you to want better. A down to earth story.

Eva Dalgety

A lot of people have come forward already to talk about their experience. However, there are still many out there who still can't. This book is for you.

Rex Olivar

Great woman, excellent lady, mother and friend. Carrol you are such an inspiration to those that know you. A woman of patience, perseverance and determination. You made a noble decision never to let circumstances boss over you, but boss over circumstances that have come to try you.

The spirituality side that you belong to can never be paralleled. The Almighty, is Alpha and Omega. He began it in you and He will see you through. Greater is He who is in you than He who is in evolution. Great work and a great model!

Joseph Muchina

PREFACE

SURVIVOR: a summary

Fight back! Fight back against whom? Authority structures especially when their values are not worth the paper it's written on: '**children should be seen and not heard**' now where does that come from? Does this come from the view held by parents who are out of touch with the needs of their own children? Not listening? Not bothering to take time to respond to their emotional needs as they make the transition from childhood through to adolescence?

This book is not only about **fighting back**; in the same breath, it is also about taking the fight in our own hands. For instance, the opening chapters without a wasted moment, seize the opportunity to draw upon my mum on the receiving end of thud! thud!! thud!!! from the high-powered fists of a husband albeit father figure with no mercy; all because he's come home from the day job to find the food not ready and the boiling pot still a long way off! Like a lamb to the slaughter, a mother is impaled and bruised day in day out to the point of ending-up in Accident & Emergency hospital until **one day** yes?

One day as my dad raises his big heavy fists, he is interrupted by the throwing of a massive stone hurled by my older brother on the behalf of all nine of us: **Leave my mother alone** (!!!) the stone narrowly missing his face thus injuring his arm and guess what? From that day onwards, he never dared lay a finger on my mum because he knew full well he would be dealing with the wrath of all of his siblings?

Taking the fight in my hands when apprehended by some big hefty gal from out of nowhere: coming to school for nothing but to taunt me and punch hell out of me evening after evening so each night I cry myself to sleep until one day yes? One day I couldn't believe she came in my own yard on my own turf to fight me then what? *Inside something so strong* this was the one battle I had to win on my own: my God my God: **this was the first diplomatic victory in my life yes**?? After de gal was given a disgraceful beating running away with her clothes in her hands, she never ever laid a finger on me again –**thank you Jesus**!

Fighting back when by the age of seventeen, with little or no career prospects, all of us in accord with the rule of our parents, had to leave home in order to survive at the hands of those who couldn't care less! By 21, my church sister the Principal of a school offered me a job to teach basic Maths and English to the kindergartens in effect coinciding with meeting the very first love of my life! Leading to total betrayal from my 15-year-old sister engaging in secret with the same man I was in love with. The shame of getting pregnant and finding myself embroiled in controversy and condemnation from sectors within the church!
It seems what I was fighting against was an institution advocating love and understanding yet when it came to a crucial situation where I am pregnant for a man outside

wedlock, there was no love and understanding! The only saving grace was more like a visiting Evangelist (Vanessa Anderson) making an impassioned plea for souls to come to the alter to be prayed for. That night she whispered a special message in my ear: *"The Lord says to tell you He has forgiven you"* which has kept me going ever since!

Years later, far removed from my Jamaican homeland, out of nowhere, a woman uses the term **"SPIRITUAL DISCRIMINATION"** to identify a particular reaction posed by my church membership: **"You have two big daughters, one dark one and a chubby brown one. God says to tell you He loves you. Do you drive?"** No sooner I answered yes, she led me to her car boot filled with groceries coinciding with my very hour of need no less than the Sunday when I was enduring all sorts of torment from within the ranks of my church how can I ever forget?

To date I am having to challenge all possible misconceptions I have ever had of love? When in all honesty, the love of every single man I have ever met, has turned to nothing more than lust of the flesh and betrayal compounded by a pack of lies.

Washing our dirty linen in public, is like taking a man to Court better still taking the Church to Court to see who holds the balance of probability –them or me?. Reading this book from cover to cover, you may well come to the conclusion that all have fallen short of the glory of God.

The church for all its worth is only a body of people: stripped to the bone, we're talking about individuals; before God we stand or fall; coming together as a conglomerate, we can't possibly agree on everything so yes, there is going to be an element of politics *did somebody say politics*? And that is at the core of everything. How often have we heard of divisions and re-grouping? No different from any other pressure group.

In all of this I have had to fight in order to maintain my sanity. If it wasn't for God and His Divine love where would I be today? Gone, lost, buried and forgotten? What of my children? I dare say, they have got their own story to tell. Right now *as for me and my house, we will serve the Lord*!

- ***Carrol Rowe***

CONTENTS

- Chapter 1 -

QUAGMIRE OF A LONESOME ROAD

I was reared and bred in Jamaica by my parents amidst the buzzing industrial complex of Kingston, the capital city until it was time for us to move to Spanish Town some fourteen miles away. I was a six year old then.

I am third of a family of nine children –three sisters and five brothers. Two boys first, then me. So you can imagine how great the expectations from my parents were. From an early age, I would be assigned to assist in the upbringing of the younger ones. There were times when I might even be stopped from school for the same reason. To be honest, I enjoyed looking after them; for me, the big sister role was more like a duty. Some may dispute the notion of someone so young, giving up valuable school hours if needs be, to ensure that one's little brothers and sisters were OK -a feature of Caribbean life I dare say!

With mom unemployed, dad would be considered sole provider and bread winner. His nature of work involved driving long distances to deliver parcels and such items. This meant leaving home from as early as 4:00am not to be seen again until 10:00 at night. In my opinion, he had a fairly good job; the Company he worked for, upgraded his status by allowing him the privilege of becoming a private contractor. This made him more financially independent and secure.

The emotional state of life as we experienced it, was based on: **FEAR** in the sense that he ruled with a rod of iron! Putting it another way, I came from a dysfunctional family where mum and dad were always quarrelling. At times as the thundering blast of his voice escalated to fever pitch of raw anger, all of us knew what was coming next. **Thud! Thud!! Thud!!!** Hitting mum with heavy hand as if she had no feelings whatsoever, and she like a lamb to the slaughter, would not even as much as retaliate. Bringing with it, no less than a pall of fear soaking into our hearts and minds day after day and night after night.

One of the main reasons underlying the spate of violence dished out by dad against mum is to do with the length of time she took to prepare food. All of us children used to comment amongst ourselves: **"Mum taking her time to peel food and put in the pot...hours and hours to wait and still, no end in sight? By the time the food was ready, the appetite was gone!"**

Yet another worrying issue, was the fact that mum was not exactly the best dressed in the house. Always looking the worst for wear, largely because dad flatly refused to look after her. Mum kept having babies every year –One baby each year might well be a contributing factor to her low self-esteem and lack of confidence in the way she presented herself. In her own eyes, feminine attraction was no big thing. If any of us girls tried to look our best she would be more inclined to tell-us-off –*sey a man we a look*!

The bottom line in all this was that dad loved loads and loads of money but was a mean spender. Would not spend on his children's education let alone budgeting for his wife to go out and buy fashionable clothes to look nice; Spending the bulk of his money on house-building projects. i.e. starting with a two-bed roomed extended to the likes of a grand ten-apartment house.
Just the sound of his voice was enough to make me recoil in anguish to realise that the world was such a cruel place. With it came a pall of loneliness. For a start, I didn't have many friends I guess because I was shy and insecure. i.e. not enough confidence to approach people. This made me sad and unloved. I had never had a cake, or a card for instance, never mind parents saying happy birthday! This was how cold my environment was; wrongly or rightly, I came to the conclusion that they didn't want me. In my family, there was no bonding between parents and children; all I can remember is continuous fighting. To be honest, they were there but not there.

I hope any reader of these pages will understand where I am coming from? Our parents were not concerned about our emotional needs however hurtful or painful. Putting it flatly, we were left to our own devices rather like being left to the mercy of the world. My dad was a disciplinarian and would be there to administer the strap at any cost. If we did wrong, he would be the first to put us back in line. With him, there was no mercy –just a cold, heartless, brutal figure of a miserable man; once you've crossed his path, that's it you've had it.

One of the worst examples of harsh treatment meted out to one of my brothers remains in living memory till this day: Dad having lost two dollars hastily came to the conclusion that my brother was the culprit. Without even questioning us properly, he proceeded to dish out punishment accordingly. At the time I was 7 years old and it pained my heart to see what my so-called Christian of a dad did to my 9 year old brother: a punishment such as to warrant parental arrest by Police if only they knew the excessive extremes to which he went –I can't print it? What upset me more than ever, was to see the helpless figure of a mother with no influence, begging and pleading to no avail. One child each year bringing the total to nine with not even as much as the courage to stand up to him!

She seemed so helpless, fragile and timid; this was due to her being uneducated and totally dependent on the iron rule administered by him. For instance, if he came in from work and found things not to his suit (i.e. dinner not ready), he would start a quarrel with mum; before we knew it **Boof! Boof!! Boof!!!** with his fists!!! On a number of occasions as I watch my mother bleed, it was bad enough to land her in the Accident & Emergency dept. Most times I would accompany her to give moral support.

Every day I kept wondering when this would end; the truth is, it didn't. There is a song that says *'children live what they learn'*, and that is a true saying. As years roll over, I watch my elder brothers grow to teenage and begin to retaliate against my Dad. One night more than all, my eldest brother now 16, lashed out at him just as he raised his hand to hit mum.

I saw him reach for a brick crying out **“YOU BETTER LEAVE MUM ALONE”**, with the brick landing on his right hand narrowly missing his face. His hand remaining in a sling for days. From that day onward, he never ever raised his hand to hit mum.

- Chapter 2 -

HELL INSIDE THE HOUSE AND HELL OUTSIDE THE HOUSE

I thought going to school would offer a way of escape from the trauma and trying times adduced to a hostile environment; but it wasn't to be; out of nowhere, this one girl took it upon her own head to mock and jeer and taunt me every single day after school. As though that wasn't enough, ensured she gave me a good beating by the time I got home. Night after night what could I do except cry myself to sleep?

At the time, I was slim and petite in appearance, with long, shoulder-length hair –a pretty girl, as some newspaper reporters might term it. As a 13-year-old, I was on the verge of finishing Primary school. In the eyes of young men, it seemed I was gradually becoming an attractive prospect, so much so they would chant a special name of endearment. i.e. *Miss Frazers Content.* The climate of intimidation carried over from my home life, would make me less confident of walking the streets on my own in case I became the subject of male predators.

I say *predators* because I used to be accosted by two brothers one of whom was a notorious gunman living in my community. Both were making it clear they fancied me - bouy wasn't I feisty! Giving them not even an inch of ground all I knew, I was defending myself, since I had no dad to stand up for me. Most times I managed to escape their advances. Following an altercation between them and the Police, sadly enough, the more notorious of the two got shot –may he rest in peace!

SCHOOL BULLYING

Too big for her size, this **big, hefty gal** as Jamaicans would term it, was more of a thorn in the flesh a nuisance if you pardon my expression! Night after night crying myself to sleep didn't help; day was dawning fast when I would have to confront her for my evening beatings; no means of escape! Looking rather like a fifteen year old, the size of her was so intimidating one just needed to see the menacing outline of a fat flabby body. From a distance she looked disgusting as if up to no good.

The only buzz she needed to feed her bullying instinct was that of pouring scorn on how small and insignificant I looked; Most days I would lock myself in the school's outside toilet for hours just to avoid her. During lunch hour I needed food to keep my strength up, so I had to eat under pressure. Knowing full well that there was no method of complaint that made sense. Once school was over and I was off the premises that's it; **The Bull Dog** of a **big hefty gal** was free to savage me. Once she started to beat me, none of the children would pull her off-me. Ha! H!! Ha!!! They saw it as entertainment!

Tattered, devastated and broken, I would be asking myself when I got home, Lord, what have I done to deserve this? Why is this girl picking on me and not someone her size? Certain mornings whilst on my way to school, she would antagonise me in a way as to incur feelings of dismay and despair so much so I felt like I'd much prefer to die than live. At no point can I ever remember my mother having any idea of what I was going through -too consumed with her own problems to notice mine. Going through the throes from day to day, my lot was nothing but **pure hell** I ended up thinking what a horrible life to live!

One day my brother who was at another school decided to wait for me after school and was just in time to see **de big hefty gal** about to give me my daily walloping. There was a heap of gravels in the school yard and out of no where I saw him on top heaping up two handfuls and starting to stone her. She ran away when she saw gravels coming thick and fast; realising now he was serious. From that day she decided to leave me alone. Thank goodness, what a relief!

The break I got from her wasn't long before she started harassing me again; this girl was determined to add more grief to my life by waiting at the school gate every evening -her behaviour becoming so intense that my brother had to wait for me everyday. By now I realised there was no escape for me. My brother loves to fight. He was willing to take her on given he is a year older than me - deciding to do what he does best, **throwing stones**. Good heavens man; you could see her running like a **big, hefty blob**. **The bull dog** stayed far from me after that day when she realised my brother wasn't joking.

IN MY OWN HOME SHE CAME TO BEAT ME!

This time it was on my turf better still, my own home ground. Now I realised **this was a battle I had to win**. Rather like David and Goliath. I likened her unto Goliath because she was bigger than me. Meaning she had broad shoulders, big busts and stockily built like a fat lump. On the contrary, I saw myself as *little David*, since I was slim, petite and tiny. At the time I weighed only ninety eighty pounds, she approximately one hundred and fifty pounds. At 13 I was so much smaller than a 15 year old sporting such a body making her look older than her age!

I was in my almond tree one day eating almond; and out of no where she appeared with verbal abuse and name calling. i.e. **"skinny like a shrimp."** In Jamaica we would say, **"little and wingy"**. Obviously counting on the fact that I was small in statue, it seemed body shapes was a big issue for her. All she was really trying to say was **"GET LOST! YOU DON'T COUNT!!"** In God's world, personality had no place; all she saw was a physical body. In my eyes, no devil can take away what God has given me, not even a bully such as her.

Trying to ignore all of this at first, I was baffled by her bold extremes. How can she take it upon herself to venture into my own space to bully me, how dare her! Still paying no attention, I dismissed her as sick in the head this isn't real? When she realised her verbal abuse wasn't getting anywhere she suddenly started throwing stones now **that was the lat straw!** In my head, I positioned my state of mind to win this fight. This is my home for a start; **Little and Win-jy** I might be; fat and useless pure noise she might be. One thing I knew for sure: nobody from out-a-road wasn't going to come een a my yard fe beat me!

ACTION TIME

AS I CLIMED DOWN FROM THE TREE, FEAR MINGLED WITH COURAGE, **TOOK HOLD OF ME** -still not knowing what would happen? She was staring at me and I was out- staring her to the point of feeling intimidated by her size one mind telling me she is going to tear me to pieces. Another mind saying **TODAY IS THE DAY TO PUT AN END TO MY YEARS OF MISERY, AND NOBODY WAS GOING TO HELP ME NOT EVEN MY BROTHER!**

Standing before her buoy wasn't that scary? My heart started pumping, cold bumps and sweat started to wash my whole body. I grabbed her hair, then started to bite her, I kicked wildly and all I heard myself saying **"YOU THINK ME FRAID A YOU GAL?"** (Courage helping me to stand my ground).

The fight was well under way to tell you the truth, I didn't realise I had so much strength. I fisted and fisted her chest and waist umpteen times with lightning speed until we both fell to the ground. This gave me an ideal vantage point whilst sitting on top of her. I grabbed her hair thus flashing her head from side to side with no mercy. **"What did you call me Gal? Eh?? Eh??? What did you call me???"** continuing to bombard her with a barrage of fists, left, right and centre.

Out of nowhere my eldest brother waded in but was restrained by one of the neighbours saying **"Leave it Paul, Carrol will deal with it"** all I could hear from the bystanders was **"GO CARROL GO!!! !!!**

Fists of electric, fighting like a giant till I noticed her blouse and skirt were getting ripped to shreds to the tune of **YES!!!**. she was beginning to feel embarrassed. Suddenly there came an old lady from out of nowhere beating and slapping us, **"GO HOME TO YOUR PARENTS!** Amidst the cheering crowds, the demon started running away with ripped blouse and skirt in hand. So much so that from that day onwards, she never laid a finger on me.

- Chapter 3 -

PARENTS' LACK OF VISION FOR OUR EDUCATION

At sixteen, I was advancing in grades and my teachers thought I had the potential to do well academically so they decided on having an audience with my parents to discuss my educational future. I was timid to give any such message to my Dad since he was unapproachable. Also, I already knew the answer he would give ***(i.e. he has to go to work and wouldn't be prepared to lose a day's pay)***. This is what he told all of us from day one, so that his stubborn refusal to support us educationally led to our downfall. Our future was taken away from us because we had parents who never cared enough to sacrifice so we could achieve. All the teachers wanted to know from my Dad is, what assistance he could offer in respect of preparing for the National CXC exams.

Where was Mum in all this? Indeed one might well ask. Like I said in the first place, she was powerless, and that was because she wasn't educated; she had little say in how money was spent in the house. All he saw her as, was a house wife –weak, powerless and lacking in the vision and inspiration to express herself on our behalf.. Such is the cruelty of my father's regime, so much so, his final words in response to our educational future was: **"TELL TEACHER IF SHE CAN GIVE ME A DAY'S PAY, THEN I WILL COME AND SEE HER!!!"**

Speaking about my parents not showing concerns or getting involved in my education or anything that concerns me. Remembering been part of the Friendship Primary School Folk dance group and use to enter competitions and not having any of my parents present. This made me feel left out, abandon and rejected. This time my dad could be forgiving because, I didn't expect him to stop from work to come watch me dance. At least mum could show some effort by giving me that moral support but she never showed up.

Under the circumstances, I had only one chance left which was the Secondary School Exam, so I made good use of it. Many days dad would send me to school without lunch money or taxi fare making it clear he hadn't got any money, yet would secretly ensure my younger sister's daily expenditure was met. This, although instilling feelings of rejection, made me all the more determined to push towards my goal; incidentally, a friend of mine was so kind, she shared her lunch with me –to date, I think she resides in Florida.

Graduation Day was approaching fast: this was the day every parent would want to make memorable for their child or children. Sadly, I didn't hold out much hope for parental involvement except for making it known that I needed a special dress for the occasion. Whatever made dad decide to ask his sister in America to send a dress left me baffled. Incidentally when the parcel arrived it the ugliest white lace frock I had ever seen in my life. When I asked for a belt to make the dress look nicer, he roared: **"EVERYTHING YU SEE PEOPLE WID YU WANT!"** Wow! What more could I ask for? Mind you, a good neighbour from next door stepped in to ensure I had a belt for the Big Day.

Speaking of Graduation Day, when parents crammed every inch of space outside and inside just to catch a glimpse of their loved ones, my own parents chose not to be present.

LIFE AFTER GRADUATION

The only jewels in the crown I could hang on to, was the results of three subjects at Secondary level: passes in Catering, English and Maths which made my teachers proud. Life after Graduation became a struggle because I was cheated out of taking the CXC National Certificate which would have led to Higher Education hence putting me in a better position to apply to College or University. I must admit that school life was exciting because I saw it as an escape route from the turmoil of home life. As a student my teachers could rely on me to produce good work.

Leaving school as a 17-year-old, was when reality hit me. Facing life alone with no one to offer Careers Advice or moral support, made matters worse. In terms of personality development, I was a shy girl unable to look people in the eye. Looking back, the bullying may have contributed to this shyness. Not managing to secure the basic qualifications I really wanted, left me feeling like an empty space –a void which could never ever be filled. As I got older, I noticed something happening which I couldn't explain: fear deeply embedded in me, yet counterbalanced by a feeling of optimism which was hard to explain; like being locked in isolation. I was feeling trapped as if something or someone was trying to suppress my inner being.

Feelings of psychological imprisonment escalated over months and years. All I did was to lock myself indoors peeping through windows as if I didn't want to be around people. The slightest quiver of tension arising if someone passed by worse someone with whom I was familiar with. One day as I drew near the mirror to take a closer look at myself, I noticed my entire features changed (given I'm a fair-complexioned person), I was turning to dark brown. Putting it simply, I was ill and no one knew, not even my parents. I guess they were too busy arguing and fussing and fighting!

There were times when my whole body tightened as the blood struggled to circulate, so much so, it wasn't until I came to the UK that my condition was properly diagnosed and yes, I was suffering from Hyperactive Thyroid. Symptoms like shortness of breath, helped the doctors to explain what I was suffering from - confirmation came after my GP ordered a blood test which confirm Hyperactive Thyroid. Were there any links between the subculture of domestic violence and bullying experienced in Jamaica? This for me, was a real question to find answers to.

- Chapter 4 -

CHURCH: what of spiritual support?

Finding myself a new skill or social group, might well be the answer to some of my problems. This goes without saying all of us are on a journey and we need some kind of spiritual support. In my quest to get more out of life, I turned my attention to the church. I started attending services at a local church. The services were great. I wanted to enjoy being around people of faith. Week after week I would be sitting in the congregation feeling all tense and nervous. I can recall a particular day when I was asked to read the Bible. There and then, I felt as if I wanted to die. ***"How am I going to face the audience?"*** an inner voice quietly whispered. Some how I convinced myself I could do it. ***"It's alright, it's not that difficult. Look straight ahead without having any eye contact".***

As I started, I realised I was crying: it wasn't that I couldn't read, it's just that **"THING"** that had a hold on me with full determination to hold me captive so yes, **THAT DAY I WAS A DISASTER!** I then decided to try another way to deal with this monster. For instance, I thought becoming part of a social group (i.e. the choir), would help me overcome psychological barriers so I could do the things I'd like to do. Somehow, I came to identify that monster as **"FEAR"**. Rather like an individual confronted by a Policeman: just about the worst thing he could ever say is "**I AM GOING TO ARREST YOU**" so that my quest at the end of the day, is to overcome this arresting spirit come what may.

FINAL BREAK: Leaving home at 17

I was a believer because one thing my dad never forgot to do, was to send us to church even though we couldn't see that it doing him any good. It was good for us to be introduced to church as we needed that source from above which had always been keeping me throughout my teenage life, especially growing up in an environment such as mine.

At 17, I started attending youth meetings and that helped a lot; With the help of specific Bible passages, I would apportion certain sections for daily reading. Also, I would talk to the Lord through prayer. In real terms, I was depending on my faith to carry me through. Getting myself baptised was one way forward. From then on, I was convinced I needed to surrender my life to Jesus and let him take full control. More than ever, I needed a safe haven –something or someone –on whom to unload my burdens thinking this would be a way out of the doldrums of a childhood past, riddled with despair.

My best laid plans were now about to coincide with a cardinal rule laid down by my father to the effect that all his children must leave home once they reach the age of 17 –hence the opening-up of a new era –this is called SURVIVAL!

- Chapter 5 -

MUDDY WATERS ROUGH AND MEAN

My dad told his sister that the only use my sister and I had, was **FOR HER TO USE US**. In my estimation, that was **HARSH, CRUEL, MEAN** and **UGLY** for him to say this in respect of his own flesh and blood. The reason I say **UGLY**, is because that was **ABUSE** and **ABUSE** is ugly.

Finding myself and my sister thrown on to two successive aunts, made me feel shameful, degraded next to an outcast. This particular Aunt I was now with, was of wealthy stock, domineering and abusive of her status. For instance, when she gave us a pile of white shirts to wash, if they weren't washed properly, she'd throw them in the dirt demanding us to re-wash them. Also, she used to give me the detergent that was supposed to be used in the washing machine telling me to use my hands to do the washing.

Also, by the time she came home, we had to make sure not a speck of dust was on the furniture else we would be woken up out of our beds to go and re-dust – I felt like a slave may God help us to forgive her. Out of frustration, it wasn't long before I ended up back with my parents. Even then, I wasn't coping very well, so I visited a second cousin of mine, a baker who used to deliver pastry to the school cafeteria.

He was a single man living with his two children and a nanny. I thought it would be safe for me since he was a preacher and preachers are respectable people who look after the needy. I was in shock: it wasn't long after I was in the bedroom when he came to talk to me. Whilst talking, I realised he was coming closer and closer. I became defensive and in no time, he reached over and grabbed me, placed me across his legs and slapped me on my bottom saying **"COUSIN AND COUSIN BOIL GOOD SOUP !"**

Even though I was young and naive, I'm sure I was no fool hence with swift decision, I packed my things and went back home.
My Dad now gave me an ultimatum: If I wanted to sleep with my younger sister, I would have to pay a hundred and fifty dollars monthly rent. On the other hand, if I wanted to rent a room, the rent would be four hundred dollars. My only alternative since four hundred dollars is a lot of money, was to hide under the bed night after night.

Since I couldn't contain this life for much longer, I went to the Minister of my church to enquire if he knew of any church member who could offer accommodation. In response there was a church sister who was going away to Canada and needed someone to look after her three children 17, 11 and 6, so yes I embraced this opportunity which worked well for a time until psychological problems developed between the 17 year old who didn't wish to be spoken to by me given that we were practically in the same age group, so for an ideal solution, this arrangement was short-lived.

- Chapter 6 -

MY FIRST LOVE

For reasons to do with emotional support, I decided to turn my attention to a young man during a crucial time of my life. This left me with a questions: "Was this a prelude to my spiritual death?" , Knowing full well that the surge of emotional needs was ever so strong within me, and the attraction between us was spontaneous. The nature of this relationship was of such as to awaken feelings, call it infatuation I don't know. What else?

At that time I was twenty-one and he, five years older. **ROGER WAS THE IDEAL MAN OF MY DREAMS**. This is not his real name but a made up name.In terms of stature, he was five feet nine, carrying a good body weight of about sixteen stones, enough to earn himself the pet name **"BULK- MAN"**. His eyes were big and bold; Clean shaved, well dressed and well presented. Not only was he academically qualified but skilled in terms of a trade. He was an electrician. For want of family background and status, he was opposite to me in the sense of hailing from a family of good values and sound educational standing he being the youngest of siblings living at home with his parents.

Roger's attraction towards me, started back there in my childhood when as an Electrician, he was employed by my dad to come and carry out electrical work whilst the building of our house was in progress. Contact (in secret) from his beady bold eyes had never failed to awaken my earliest responses to learn to value and respect his presence! So much so as years rolled over, a deep-seated, and binding attraction was the end product.

THE BLOSSOMING OF LOVE

When Roger first saw me, I COULD FEEL THAT HE LOVED ME THEN. He knew the pressures I was under, better still, he saw my need for emotional support which is why he turned out to be so protective; hence, in the long run making me feel secure and trusting of him. To me, it was an honour to be invited to his home to meet his parents and rest of siblings. This did much to my own personal self-esteem. Given that it took years for me to reach this point.

My first real job as Kindergarten Teacher instilled a freshness and newness of experience in the sense that it was the job satisfaction for money and material things. **WHAT GAVE ME THE 'BUZZ' WAS ROGER ASSUMING VIRTUALLY FULL CHARGE OF MY LIFE**. Most evenings he would come to meet me on my way from school. Believe it or not, our most valued and cherished moments were spent in his bedroom at his parent's home; comprising lavishing upstairs and downstairs apartments. So yes our 'love nest' was downstairs.

PSYCHOLOGICAL CONFLICT

Still for all of this, my mind was not at ease; spending quality time in the privacy of his bedroom was probably not the best way forward since the closer we got, the more physical our demands! We wanted to be locked in each others' arms so as to be entwined for ever and ever. Even the closeness of our breath in utter silence told its own story -how intimate can we get? Day or night made no difference. At times we went too far and this was beginning to worry me. Mingled with all of this I couldn't help feeling strands of gratitude welling-up inside my body. Up till this time, **NOBODY HAD EVER MADE ME FEEL LOVED AND WANTED LIKE THIS MAN!**

WHAT AM I DOING WITH AN UNSAVED MAN? As a Christian this is the question I was lumbered with. What is this doing for my status within the church community? At the time I was resident at the home of a church sister, surely there must have been times when she became concerned about my absence especially if I happened to be sleeping over. What of my commitment to values upheld by the church? My difficulties in engaging Roger on any level of discussion to do with Bible or Religion was another source of worry -could I get him to listen? No way, he'd just change the subject at random. So now I was torn with the decision to let go of this man and come clean -easier said than done!

Given that my childhood years had been besieged by a catalogue of harsh treatments, why did a loving God allow such abuse to befall me? Day after day I wrestled with these thoughts because I wasn't willing to walk away from a man who gave me as much nurturing as to make me feel wanted and loved; after all **ROGER WAS MY FIRST LOVE**! It was hard for me to give him up just for the sake of conscience.

As a Christian girl, I thought perhaps I should have had the good sense to balance both church and love life. But then I was only fooling myself: Roger was as stubborn as an ox, he wasn't going to walk with me on any Christian path.

WEB OF DECEPTION

Back to earth once again to face reality was no joke! In admitting my own limitations I was beginning to see how foolish and naive I was. For all I care, this was telling me how little I knew of the outside world let alone men. What do they want? As an innocent and trusting young woman (to the point of thinking all that glitters is gold), I had to learn the hard way. Coming to the realisation that the whole thing was a trap that the devil was setting and I was about to fall into it.
By the time I was on the verge of getting out I was already drawn into the web. Stands to reason that Roger's amazing masculine frame, his bold bright eyes and his charm were just for a season -and the season was about to expire! Roger was the web and I became the spider (hence, the moral of the story), i.e. **ONCE YOU FALL INTO THAT WEB, GOD HELP YOU IF YOU CAME OUT ALIVE!**

Deep deep down, I knew I should not have taken his bedroom for sanctuary nor give him the wonderful satisfaction for which he craved. After all he wasn't serious: Moreover, he knew what he was doing. The devil was using him to tarnish my innocence and leave me confused. He was the man with the words to blind me with science; **ALL HE WAS AFTER WAS A BIT OF FUN ('smiles')**.

Deep deep down I knew what I wanted. For instance, it takes a strong Christian to fend off sugar-coated confidence tricksters looking for a relationship by laying ground rules such as **NO SEX BEFORE MARRIAGE!!!** In drawing upon my own short-comings and limitations with respect to educational and financial needs, he was well placed to take advantage of my situation. **AFTER FIVE MONTHS OF FOOLING AROUND, I SUDDENLY REALISED I WAS PREGNANT**. This now caused me to move out of my church sister's house, because she wasn't prepared to tolerate and uphold the lifestyle I was living!

SPIRITUAL DEATH

Spiritual death for me meant two things:walking away from the believers to hook up with a man who is completely outside the Church family and the other is that of conceiving a child for him - in common law terms would be called 'living in sin' hence my question: **WHERE IS MY KNIGHT IN SHINING ARMOUR? WHAT WERE HIS THOUGHTS AT THIS TIME? WOULD HE BE PREPARED TO COME FULL CIRCLE AND OFFER TO MARRY ME?** This probably would have been a giant step to help alleviate my shame -alas not a chance! To be fair, there was marginal acceptance of fatherhood yet he had no ambition to engage in efforts to purchase a house preferring me if worse came to the worse, to lodge with his parents inside the one-room.

DIVINE FORGIVENESS

At last, a precious moment of spiritual and psychological relief came when a visiting Evangelist from Canada -Vanessa Anderson - came to address my local Church. Venturing into the building, I thought it safe to sit at the last back given the state of mind that my sins might find me out (?). The Holy Ghost in my estimation, was speaking through her that night as the final stages of an Alter Call came. Virtually everyone went up to be prayed for except me! In my confused state, I heard her say **"you at the back come here!"** 'Earth O Earth', I wished the whole earth could open and take me in". Tentatively, I made my way towards the platform; Then slowly walking away from the microphone, she whispered **"YOU KNEW WHAT YOU HAVE DONE, BUT GOD HAS FORGIVEN YOU!"** Those words alone from that moment onwards, gave me enough strength to face a whole barrage of criticisms right the way to the very moment when I gave birth to my child.

The bulk of these criticisms carried very little by way of love and understanding. Till this day, I give thanks for the whispering words of the visiting preacher; had it not been for the forgiveness expressed by God through her, I don't know where I would be today.

- Chapter 7 -

WHEN LOVE TURNS SOUR

As I became pregnant yet again by Roger, thoughts of returning to the Church family, dawned on my mind. Mind you, the only way this was going to happen was if he decided to come full clear on the subject of whether he wanted to marry me or not.

During his teens, he was active in church and Sunday school. What are his thoughts on fatherhood and raising a family? This was something he was passionate about in fact, going to great lengths to advise me on having -what Jamaicans describe as - **a 'bush bath'** for the purpose of warding-off the effects of witchcraft on our unborn child. Given that my stance was 'superstitious', I had no choice in the matter but to co-operate.

At long last, we were blessed with the joyous occasion of the birth of our second baby girl, and I thought Roger would be over the moon but no, the opposite! He seemed on edge, touchy as one might say; If fly brushed past, he would erupt into cursing and swearing; at the impulse of light conversation he was ready to lash-out; before you know it, b'doom! boof! boof!

I was trying to find the underlying cause for these mood swings. Like I've said, he was kind, gentle and loving right up to the birth of our baby –why now is this sudden change? For instance, if he saw me talking to a passer-by particularly of the opposite sex, he'd be jealously assuming something is going on between us. With fist fights becoming commonplace, the onus was on me to defend myself. I wasn't going to stand-up and **mek him b'doom! boof! boof in other words throw punches at me!** Anything I could find **fe lik him dung** as some Jamaicans would say -either he or me: I was determined not to take any nonsense from him.

I remember asking my mum if she could assist us with child care which would free me up to get back into education and study life, but she told me flatly she had done enough to raise her siblings and wasn't prepared to do any more. In desperation, I turned to my 15-year-old sister who was all I had -she was a 'God send'! In one of her frequent visits, I remember us playing dominoes. Time was far spent; **"GO HOME NOW, I THINK IT'S GETTING RATHER LATE"**, I told her.

THE TRUTH UNVEILED

Asking my sister to go seemed to touch a raw nerve; the man's body-language changed in an instant! Voice erupting into frenzy, with layers of gravel tone, he rolled his big, naked, bold, eyes at me as he started throwing punches right, left and centre: **"BRING HER BACK; I AM GOING AFTER HER UNTIL I AM GOOD AND READY TO WALK HER HOME!"**

Totally confused by his level of bullying, I instantly agreed, leaving a trail of unanswered questions: yes, she's my sister, yes she's fifteen years old, yes she's the only family support I have since mum has flatly refused to help with childcare so what's this? **WHY IS THIS MAN SO CONCERNED ABOUT MY SISTER'S WELL BEING?** From the dark corners of my mind, I quickly dismissed notions of deep friendship developing between them. Suspicions burned deeply within my stomach and I couldn't help searching his trousers only to find a letter secreted in the inside pocket **'YOU ARE MINE'** in my own sister's handwriting -this was when the penny dropped!!!

Betrayal -a double betrayal at that: How could a Big Man approaching his 30's stoop so low? What can a fifteen-year-old do for him? What was my sister thinking when she wrote such words? Right in my face! This left me so furious and embittered that I had to challenge him. He was humble as a lamb doing his level best to assure me there was nothing going on between my sister and him; he didn't take the letter seriously, moreover, he would never do anything to hurt me.

Tension escalated between me and Roger to the point where I decided my sister was no longer welcome to our home and if she did, would have to leave early. As a matter a fact according to Roger his mother told him that when I am not there she can come to the house. My question is; "Does she love her grandchildren?" I guess this didn't work because he planned alternative ways of hitting-it-off with her. For instance, pretending to be working every day especially week-ends. Everything was in place; he knew very well where the love nest was going to be. Turning up late night after night, never without an excuse, took me to the point where I started dis-believing Roger again. I guess this didn't work because he planned alternative ways of hitting-it-off. He had something up his sleeve. For instance, pretending to be working every day especially week-ends. On that note I decided to wonder should I end the relationship or should I stay?

CAUGHT IN THE VERY ACT!

For the reader of this page, let me take you back to the beginning of the chapter where I am identifying my baby father's mood swings especially after the birth of our second child. Weeks leading up to the birth, he was doing his level best to balance a relationship between my sister and me, hence, leaving him in an awful quagmire of guilt. To prove my point, I was admitted into hospital for several days to be treated for high blood pressure, and this is where he and my sister seized the opportunity to take control over my home. She, despite my orders not to stay late, was now sleeping over. Can you believe this?

Following the birth of my second daughter and immediate discharge from hospital well past 8:00pm, she boldly offered to sleep-over to assist with childcare. While I occupied the bedroom they were in the sitting room for hours on end. Shock-after-shock as I scrambled to the sitting room to have a quiet word with Roger. As I pushed my head through the curtain separating both rooms, I noticed she was in a lying position whilst his head was down in her face. O my God, this was the last straw in terms of ultimate betrayal - **HOW**

COULD MY BLOOD SISTER DO THIS TO ME HER ELDER SISTER, HAS SHE GOT NO MORALS? “What’s going on?” his face looked like a frightened child. On impulse, I reached for a tin of baby food and pelted him in his face. **THE BEAST OF A MAN WAS SPEECHLESS** as he held down his head in utter shame.

As for my sister: She turned out to be a nasty piece of work. How evil can one be? Right in my face? Setting out to destroy the relationship between my children’s father and me? Coming to think of it, I remember Roger making a prophecy to the effect of turning the heart of my sister against me, surely enough he’s succeeded in doing just that. One may ask, **“Did your parents have any idea that their under aged daughter has been molested by this man?”** Yes I told my mum. As a matter a fact my sister was always accosted by me. My mum was aware of how hurt and angry I was towards her. She always uphold my sister in her wrong doing by attacking me and asking me , **If is eat I wanted to eat her?** Not sure what she meant because my reaction towards her was normal. She was destroying a life I was trying to build with my children’s dad. Nevertheless, he was just as guilty as her.

- Chapter 8 -

DECISION; SURRENDER; BIG FIGHT?? NO SEX???

"I want to make a full and unconditional surrender of my life before the Lord", said I to Roger.

"Come again **YOU?**

"Yes me!"

"Am I hearing correctly?"

An evangelical crusade was coming up soon. That's how the conversation started.

"YOU?"

"Yes me; YOU AND ME: COME WITH ME TO THE CRUSADE! GOD WILL BLESS YOU!"

"Yes, I am coming with you to the crusade!"

That lying two timer of a man for a moment I believed him. Anything to do with God, the Bible or Christianity, this man is as stubborn as an ox. As I looked into his big, bold, beady eyes, part of me wanted to believe him. As for the rest, I wasn't far wrong. The whole 3-day event took place up till then, no sign of him. Afterwards bombarding me with excuses. i.e. 'next-door neighbour taken ill…rushed to hospital etc, etc'.

"LISTEN: I HAVE RE-COMMITED MY LIFE TO CHRIST AND AM NOT LIVING IN SIN WITH YOU ANYMORE" –before the last word came out of my mouth-

"YOU WOT?" grabbing me up…big voice filling- up the whole room

"YU MEAN YU'RE NOT SLEEPING WITH ME ANYMORE??"

"NO", I said firmly - my heartbeat going boop, boop, boop, as he started slapping me right left and centre. Returning thump-up-thump-up, I gave as good as I got. The big strong Dragon started dragging my hair from his downstairs flat all the way upstairs to his parents' quarters. His parents crying out: "stop that now, now, now"! He was dishing-out more and more of his fiercest punches and I was mashing-up his head with more thump-up thump-up!!! !!! Old Swine... thinking that Christians can't fight; he made a big mistake that day! The flesh was ready to fight back. **THAT WAS MY WORST FIGHT EVER!!!**

This man would be happy to tear me to pieces if he saw me trying to rise above his animal passions that sever humanity from divinity., Like a sexual predator, his one mission in life is to control and limit my movements. For him, the ultimate goal is to see me writhe in bondage beneath his feet, thereby surrendering to an agenda based on greed –his own sexual greed. Equating me only with the flesh so that my role in life is to serve him! Today, I am no longer associated with his reign of terror; for this cause, I give thanks knowing full well, it could have been worst.

To end this chapter, I'd like to reflect on a frightful situation which made me aware of his cruel and sadistic demeanour. One early morning whilst giving me a lift to work –incidentally, the children were in the back – he turned the car round and started driving recklessly in the opposite direction, so before I knew it, we were on a lonely country road taking me to a place called flat bridge. This was where a road ran between both sides of a river. Backing on to the side of the road, he pulled out a knife: **"Daddy, Daddy, don't hurt mummy!**

With the knife at my throat, I was literally begging and pleading for my life! "YOU ARE LUCKY THE CHILDREN ARE IN THE CAR", he retorted.

WHERE DID THIS LEVEL OF ANGER COME FROM?

One of my other sisters was on her way to the airport and needed a lift. Earlier on in the morning during the traffic congestion Roger was trying to follow a car driven by one my work colleagues; the Presiding Administrator. I thought he might be kind enough to assist my sister by either calling a cab, or taking her straight to the airport himself. But we lost him in the rush. Clearly, In the children's father's eyes, he saw this man as a threat. ***"You have me running down your man!"*** How stupid can one be?

- Chapter 9 -

MY FIRST ENCOUNTER OF FAITH

As time went by, I was given into solitude and contemplation to the effect that I was sick and tired of a catalogue of lies, sexual manipulation, treachery, personal abuse and violence. In effect, my mind went all the way back to the visiting Canadian Evangelist –Vanessa Anderson – who gently whispered "God has forgiven you" in the face of all the church members who were castigating me right, left and centre for living a life of sin and getting pregnant out of wedlock. Taking to the words of Holy Writ, I came to the conclusion that if I confessed my sins to the Lord, He would be faithful and just to forgive me.

As such, I now made a petition to God on the basis that if my wish was granted, I would re-dedicate my life to the service of the Lord and His Church for the sake of myself and my children. I prayed this time lifting up my faith with the fullest assurance that God would answer my request and provide a major breakthrough in my life. That was the Saturday and by the Monday the door knocked: One of my brothers was outside exclaiming that my dad wanted to speak to me.
Approaching the door trembling and shaking, I was baffled to know what was he wanted to say to me with a bunch of keys.

"THIS BUNCH OF KEYS BELONG TO AN APARTMENT CONSISTING OF A MASTER BEDROOM, KITCHEN AND BATHROOM ALL UNDER ONE COVER AND A CAR PORCH ALL GRILLED".

Baffled as I was, it began to make sense the moment he mentioned my uncle from Canada: **"YOUR UNCLE CALLED AND TOLD ME WHAT YOU WERE GOING THROUGH AND THAT YOU NEEDED HELP...GO LIVE LIKE SOMEBODY!"** offering me the bunch of keys: This was my first testimony of faith and answered prayer. Through continued correspondence, my uncle had been there for me so yes, it made sense! Next day I couldn't wait to go and see this property which by the way was absolutely beautiful. Mind you the walls needed scrubbing and cleaning; to me that was no problem given a bucket of paint was already bought to start the work. All this was done in secret. i.e. like Matlock, I behaved like a private detective. On completion, I ordered a bed, dresser and stove etc, etc.

ESCAPE OR RENEWAL OF FRIENDSHIP?

My mum was about to get a break in her life and immigrated to Grand Cayman. This was how I would get away from the Dragon. Packing my suitcase with mine and my children's clothes, I hid it under the bed of the next-door neighbour. The day of mum's departure, I decided to accompany her to the airport then returned to let him know I was leaving –this time for good. As I clutched my girls to me with suitcase in hand, his face looked flushed almost numb. As a last-ditch stand, he offered to escort us to our new dwelling frankly, I don't know why I listened to him, but I did.

- Chapter 10 -

ABOUT TO BE THROWN IN THE DEEP END (my daughter seriously disturbed)

Realising now that the devil was setting out to bring confusion and destruction upon my children and me, I decided I wasn't going to let this deter me. For instance, on a normal Sunday, I would be singing in the choir in church in fact, my soprano voice helping to add an air of mellifluence especially if allocated solo parts.

In a moment of distraction I am thinking *'please God no! No not now (!!)'* as my seven-year-old daughter erupts into a violent uncontrollable outburst emitting loud screams amidst fainting, frothing and spitting. Under emergency conditions, this can be frightening. Thank God nevertheless for the love and understanding displayed by praying members forming a ring round her to plea Divine intervention to restore calm. All too often, the praise and worship would be disturbed in such unseemly manner! Most times I had to be saying to myself *'had it not been for God what would I do?'*

Time and again whilst in the day job, my schedule would be interrupted by a phone call: ***'come please and collect your daughter from the school premises -she's out of control!!!*** This went on for weeks if not months so much so I started searching for answers. **For instance, the fact that**

my fiancée had since left Jamaica for the USA in order to seek gainful employment left a void in my life would this be a factor? The last straw for want of an answer was to turn to God by fasting for three days.

MY DAUGHTER IS WHOLLY AND COMPETELY DELIVERED!!!

Following three days of fasting and prayer, the Lord said: **"THIS IS YOUR CHILD AND IT IS YOUR JOB TO DELIVER HER!!"** Realising now that my time had come to exercise faith, I decided it was going to be now or never. To be honest, this was a first time experience trying to deliver someone who was demon possessed. I wasn't going to let anyone come between my God, my daughter and me. What's more, I was given a clear mandate by Divine Intervention that this job had got to be done through me.

Realising that the Son of God was the Master Healer through me, there and then I took it upon myself to voice the name **"JESUS"** (!) with full force. e.g. sound engulfing the whole room of the house. As though that wasn't enough, I articulated the fact that **"JESUS"** (!!) was in control so much so that at the name **"JESUS"** (!!!) -saith the word - demons have got to flee. Proceeding now to lay hands on her declaring at full blast: **"COME!!! OUT!! OF!!! HER!!! AND DON'T YOU EVER** (YOU DEVIL), **DONT!!! YOU!!! EVER!!! COME!!! BACK!!!** There and then I noticed a visible change -her body laying protectively under my chin.

I noticed she was breathing slowly as in a deep rest scarcely uttering a word. As her eyes flickered, she looked away then looked into my eyes: '*God*', I quietly exclaimed, '*Thank you for Your Son Jesus Christ.* Thereafter, I blessed a cup of water and gave her to drink.

FINAL THOUGHTS ON THIS MATTER

On the surface, it looks as though witchcraft was directed at my daughter but in real terms it was for me. As a matter a fact, the man who conducted my bush bath prior to the birth of this child, was a regular visitor to the house; in so doing, part of a conspiracy to destroy my life by death. The sprinkling of the blood of a chicken was used as a sacrifice in this ritual. ***Psalm 91 says " He that dwelleth in the secret place of the Most High shall abide under the shadow of the Almighty".***

- Chapter 11 -

CLOUD NINE: BLISS AND SPLENDOUR THEN BOOF!!!

The pressure was off; my life seemed some what solitary now that I was living alone and moving on with the rest my life. One Saturday evening whilst still living in the house my dad gave me, I was on my way to a Barbecue at church.

Whilst walking to a taxi, I was approached by this guy in a car: ***"where are you going?"***. I told him I was going to a Barbecue at church so he decided to join me. From that day onwards he started visiting church until we became close friends; this led to a relationship. He became dedicated to church life and me in effect, a year passed and we were still together. He was there for me virtually, all my material needs were met. He was quiet, self retained and not too verbal. More of an action man who would see things needed doing and taking the initiative to do them; not much of a charmer, yet he reminded me so much of former Olympic Athlete Linford Christie, same height and facial features.

Taking things to the next level, we decided to get engaged. This was moving on an upward spiral of progress. He gave me the 'surprise of my life', by organising a luxurious engagement party! As though that wasn't enough, I was adorned with a most expensive diamond engagement ring - resulting in the happiest time in my whole life after all the

turmoil and trying times I had been through. I didn't know I would find someone who would cherish me, like this guy. Not only me but my two girls; loving and nurturing us almost too good to be true? We felt comfortable enough to move into his own flat if we really wanted to. On principle, I much preferred to do the Christian thing and not live together before we were married.
Little did I know this would be short lived. No sooner than my children's father heard news of my associations with this man, things turned sour whereby he would sit at a convenient vantage point to watch us pass by on a day-to-day basis.

ENTRAPPED IN A WEB OF SUSTAINED VIOLENCE!

If he saw my fiancée's car passing with the kids and me, that's the time he would pretend he needed the children. I tried to play the fool by accommodating him and his wishes just for peace sake. At times he would turn up unexpectedly without notifying me. On such occasions the atmosphere was uncomfortable. If I gave him the impression he was not welcome he would start a world war, so I tried my best to play it by ear. This man was persistently trying to make his way back into my life even though I was engaged.
Whenever he came for the girls and I went to pick them up, he would keep them inside his house and tell me to come for them assuring he wasn't going to harm me. One evening I went for them and was naive enough to believe him. No sooner I got in, he locked the door amidst threats

and bullying compounded with accusations of betrayal--ending in a big fight for example dragging me into the bathroom and shoving me into the bath. I managed to roll over, grab onto him and head for the front door, picked up a stone and pelted him severing his gold watch from his wrist. By then, he got the message I wasn't interested in him.

Things seemed fine until some months later. I was picked up by my fiancée from work and as we went to my apartment and sat on the car porch preparing for the wedding, it wasn't long before I heard an uproar outside. When I went to look, it was my children's dad. Up until this day I am not sure what wind had blown him to the apartment. All I saw was him coming at me with great force. I left my fiancée sitting over the other side of the house. As I approached the grill to close it, he got there before me. Without warning, he swung open the grill and I rushed to my big brother's room trying to get away from him: As I slammed the door, he pulled it so hard it came off the hinges. Then pushed me to the ground and started throwing punches. Amidst the fighting, my fiancée rushed over so the whole thing turned out into a three-cornered fight. After the fight I ended up in the Spanish Town Hospital. The doctor asked me what happened. I told him I was beaten up by my children's dad. After the examination the doctor concluded I had a broken coccyxs (Tail) bone.

- Chapter 12 -

DAD DECIDED TO INTERVENE

My dad realising this was a mad man needing to be disciplined, took legal action by getting one of the best Lawyers in Spanish Town to press charges. Roger was subsequently arrested and charged with assault and malicious destruction of property.

As the battle started in court, things intensified. It came a time when I needed witnesses to intervene in my defence, but no one was willing to stand by me. My sister-in-law was there and witnessed what happened that day, yet refused to testify. The situation looked bleak to say the least.

My fiancée as it happened, was my only support. He was planning to migrate to America since his mum was filing for him. 'It won't be long' -I was thinking -'before I am left to fight this battle on my own'. He had started to abuse my 15 year old sister as well. The thought of testifying against my children's dad wasn't easy but I had to do it. Else he would think it was OK for him to continue abusing both me and my sister. Abuse of a 15-year-old carries a serious charge in Jamaica. Living with him as his common-law-wife, was illegal. I had to depend on God to take me through all this.

During this difficult time, I thought my ex would adopt a neutral stance by staying away from me, since things were spiralling out of control, but only made matters worse by perpetuating his brutal campaign of personal harassment - no letting up!

I was a teacher at this time,and his cruel and sadistic behaviour took a turn for the worse. Not only did he portray bad behaviour within the community where I lived, but took to the school where I worked. During lunch hour, he would jump the gate and abduct our two girls and take them away. He would do this repeatedly only to be challenged by the Police who would rescue them and take them back to school. This went on for months even though our case was in progress with restrictions that he shouldn't come near me.

This man wouldn't stop trying to intimidate and harass me. He would find alternative ways to interrupt my schedule day after day. One day in particular whilst at school, my fiancée decided to come for me! The timing was absolutely crucial: 'Saved by the bell', as one might say! Good thing I vacated the premises else that would have been the day of my doom!

Luckily, my fiancée and I spent the entire afternoon in town before he took me back home late that evening. As we drove up to my gate, he walked me inside. My eldest brother suddenly appeared uttering the unbelievable: **"GIRL YOU ARE LUCKY TODAY BECAUSE Roger AND HIS GANG CAME ROUND HERE WITH GUNS TO KILL YOU!"**

- Chapter 12 -

SUDDEN U-TURN

Life turned in another direction. As I said earlier in my story, I wanted to get married before moving-in to live with my fiancé', but there was a dramatic turn of events Ensuring under such conditions that I wasn't left on my own unprotected, my fiancée took me to the house his mum left for him and his sisters when she migrated to America. The ultimate plan given he was filing for USA Citizenship, would be to get married and thereafter, migrate together with my children and me, to find a new life in America.

- Chapter 13 -

ALONE IN THE BATTLE

The time had come for my fiancée to start travelling and I was left to face the devil alone in the flesh. Whenever he went away he normally spent three to six months because of his job, then return to Jamaica for six months.

During this time I would be closely monitored by my ex by now he would know that I was on my own. To keep my sanity, I had to remain as firm as a rock knowing full well my trials were only just beginning; for all this, I am saying like David the Psalmist: ***"Had it not been for the Lord on my side, the enemy would have swallowed me up".***

I am a Survivor; what if the Lord in his infinite mercy was not by my side? During the battle at court with Roger, I had since been approached by several persons who told me to give up and let matters rest. One of the main persons siding with him in all his wrongs, was his mother. In my book, violence and systematic abuse should not be tolerated in a civilized society; such would be tantamount to a violation of human rights. Had she tried to plant a seed in his mind to the contrary, he would know what he was doing was wrong.

His prophecy of turning my sister's heart against me had certainly come to pass. With the practice of witchcraft, making it all the more real: this man is evil;

such notions aught not to be left unchallenged. My quest is justice must be served so yes, I was determined to show him that the walls of violence and abuse **"MUST COME DOWN"**. Somewhere in his heart of hearts, he must be made to re-think.
I didn't give up and certainly wasn't afraid of all the threats that were levelled from his mum. To be honest, I do not have a problem with his sisters, in effect, I am conscious of their continued respect throughout the whole of this dreadful saga. Sadly enough as this story reaches its climax, Roger was taken handcuffed by two Prison Officers to be incarcerated into Prison Cells for an indefinite time. What more can one say?

As weeks turned into months, the battle became more intense at times giving me no rest day or night, so much that my body was beginning to endure the strain and stress. In spirit, I was up for the fight though the flesh was weak. The tactics of the devil were designed to frustrate; for example, I remember sitting in court at the back one day when a Police Officer muttered,**"What are you doing here, you are a Christian?" Does he mean *"turn the other cheek, go home and be happy?"*** Many Christian will allow violence and abuse to be swept under the carpet -I am not one of those! My God says, ***"If anyone should hurt one of these little ones, it is best he take a milestone and hang around his neck"***

- Chapter 14 -

THE DAY OF SENTENCING!

At last, the day we all dreaded had finally come! Nobody likes to be arrested, charged and shamed-up in public let alone found guilty in an open Court in front of everybody! Worst, to be sentenced to time in prison. Bringing shame on the whole community, so in the face of public opinion, a man has made a public disgrace of himself.

I am not here to gloat on the misfortunes of others.; this wouldn't be in keeping with my mission. All I am here to advocate is that **MEN SHOULD NOT BE ALLOWED FREE REIN TO PERPETUATE LEVELS OF PHYSICAL ABUSE WITHIN THE PRIVACY OF THEIR OWN HOMES AGAINST LOVED ONES BE IT WIVES OR GIRL FRIENDS. WORSE FOR CHILDREN WHO ARE HAVING TO BEAR THE BRUNT OF BEING TRAUMATISED FOR YEARS TO COME! MOTHERS MOREOVER, SHOULD SEIZE THE OPPORTUNITY TO REPORT THESE SITUATIONS AND NOT LEAVE SUCH INHUMANE TREATMENT UNCHALLENGED!!! FINALLY, WE OWE IT TO OUR CHILDREN TO NOT DO WHAT MY MUM DID. MY OWN MOTHER LITERALLY REFUSED TO STAND UP TO MY DAD AND LET HIM KNOW THAT THIS BARBARIC WAY OF ILL-TREATMENT TOWARDS WOMEN MUST BE STOPPED!!!**

Yes, my children's father was sentenced to six months of in prison. What did I feel for this man as he was led away? What were the expressions on his face? For a moment he looked bland momentarily looking round before hanging is head in utter shame.

I remember at one point during his incarceration in jail his Lawyer called, asking me to go easy on him saying *"Prison life doesn't suit him"* -clearly he was losing weight!"

- Chapter 15 -

1998:THE ILL-FATED WEDDING

Getting married to my fiancé, didn't sit right with me, in fact I became so uncomfortable about the idea, that I decided to move out of his house and seek alternative accommodation. Before he left for America, he had high hopes of not staying too long. Once he got back, we would get married and migrate to the USA to start a new life with me and my children. No sooner than returning to Jamaica, he headed to his house only to realise I wasn't living there any more.

One Saturday afternoon whilst coming out of my friend's yard, I was so frightened when I saw him, I wanted to disappear. Naturally, he was upset with me when I told him straight I didn't want to go through with the marriage. He couldn't handle it; now persuading me in the strongest terms. **"COME BACK HOME WITH ME!"**, insisting **"I WILL KILL MYSELF IF I DON'T MARRY YOU!"**. Driving me further into confusion what more can I say except this must be true love if this man is prepared to take his own life if he doesn't get his own way.

In my hearts of hearts, I was contemplating on the word of God which says ***"Be ye not unequally yoked together with an unbeliever; what fellowship hath darkness with light?"*** **(2 Corinthians 6:14)**. Hooking-up with an unbeliever is just going to make matters worse. Bad as it sounds, I gave into his evil scheme and decided to go ahead with the marriage. No sooner than we were married, his behaviour changed radically. For instance, no plans were made for us to migrate to America for a new life. With withdrawal symptoms, he kept further and further away till he took to the aircraft for America thus leaving me in despair.

During his absence, I sought God as I got deeper into the warfare of prayer; all of this was resolved in a revelation I had in a dream about a ring. In the spirit, I saw where the ring turned into three different colours. This was a twenty-five carrot gold diamond ring from America which was heavily fixed for me with witchcraft. After raising further questions, I came to the realisation that there was a strong connection with **"De Laurence"** so the ring in effect, was a demonic trap leaving me with no alternative but to get rid of it by flushing it down the toilet. i.e. ***"In the name of the Lord Jesus Christ, I command these powers to be broken from now and henceforth!"*** Knowing full well that this man was nothing but trouble, all I was saying as he headed for the airport to go back to America was GOOD RIDDANCE! An encouragement to people of God who are expecting to be married to be aware that is not all that glitter is gold. There are people out there and are connected to cults. Please make sure you listens to the voice of God when you are seeking a spouse.

- Chapter 16 -

LIFE FROM A DIFFERENT ANGLE

When he left for America, I started evaluating my life in a way as to take charge of how I was going to move forward. Not having anyone to run to for moral support, left me at a disadvantage even though my dad came to my rescue by challenging the unacceptable behaviour of my children's father.

Psychologically, I was becoming low in spirit to the point of experiencing demonic attacks. This I thought had to do with wrong choice of partners. One day I was at home with the girls and felt sad and depressed, so I decided to send them to their dad to take time out to reflect. I guess this made matters worse so I choose to cheer up myself by playing some gospel music but the feeling wouldn't go away

I guess it was deeper than just feelings of despair. Maybe I was grieving the loss of my marriage and the traumatic experiences I had been through. For the whole day I couldn't focus clearly. Luckily a friend stopped by.. As we were talking about my feelings, she suggested that it would be a good idea to get prayed for. She mentioned that there was a crusade in a nearby community. And that we should go. I decided to take up the offer -we both went.. After the message the Minster made an alter call saying **"There is someone here tonight that they put witchcraft spells**

on and tonight is your night for God to deliver you" He further said I am going to count to ten and give you time to get to come to the front. I sat and listened hoping that somebody would get up. Unfortunately no one got up. So I said to myself I was struggling today with the feeling of oppression so let me go to the alter. As I got up and was walking towards him he said to me **"I never know you was going to get up, because when you go back home it would be you and your duppies"** The Brits would say Spirits"
As he laid his hands on me and voiced **"IN THE NAME OF JESUS, I COMMAND THE SPIRIT OF WITCHCRAFT TO BE BROKEN!!!'** All I remember is, I fell on the ground and started vomiting blood, after that phase had past I felt light. That night my friend decided I should not go back to the house, so I moved out and stayed with her until I found new accommodation.

Times were hard and my life was going downhill so yes - I decided to step out of my comfort zone in order to explore possibilities e.g. throw myself into the deep so to speak! For the first time I was actually engaging with a drama group in my local church. This helped to boost my self-confidence.

- Chapter 17 -

CLERICAL OFFICER OF FAITH: IMMIGRATION DEPT

One day, as I joined the queue at the Spanish Town Immigration Dept to apply for a passport, I waited and waited only to realise there wasn't anyone attending at the Admin Desk. So I stepped to front of queue, rang the bell and a Police Officer came forward and asked "Can I help?".

"The queue is getting longer and longer and there was no one to attend to us; what's going on?" The police officer said *There wasn't anyone permanently working in that position; the person who worked there is on holiday.* **"Can I get the position?"**, I bravely asked. I don't know where the confidence came from. *"Are you interested?"*.Looking at me with curiosity *"If you are serious, go to Spanish Town Road on Monday morning and speak to the Chief Immigration Officer at Head Office"*. I did what was suggested.

When I turned up that Monday morning and asked for the Chief Immigration Officer, a woman stepped towards me ***"Can I help you?."*** **I was at the Spanish Town Immigration Department on Friday awaiting someone to attend me, but there was no one. I enquired about the position and was told there was a vacancy that's why I am here. I was also told to come to have a talk with you".**

The Bible says ***"The righteous is as bold as a lion"***. In my heart, I was saying **"I am claiming the job in Jesus name!"** Looking rather puzzled she exclaimed ***"There are a lot of people queuing for this position, but I am going to give it to you".*** We both share the surname "Miller" In my mind, I felt this was a divine connection from heaven not a coincidence. During my job at Passport and Immigration, I met people who were backsliders and encouraged them to re-surrender their lives and return to the Lord. This was like I opened up hell's door: each time I mentioned Jesus, it was like touching a raw nerve. i.e. or opening a can of worms. I was planning to migrate to America whilst working there but things didn't materialized so I left because I thought it was time to move on. I must admit I did enjoy working there because it was a new experience for me. Also, I will never forget how I came to have gotten the job.

- Chapter 18 -

GET YOUR PASSPORT READY, YOU ARE GOING TO TRAVEL!

Drapery and Design, had now become the focus of attention. For a change, I really wanted to know what it felt like working for myself, so I bought two industrial machines and two over lockers as well as employing one person to work with me. In no time, we were making draperies and other household items and selling them to bring an income so I could look after my family.
This was how I survived until deciding to embark on a new journey of life .

Putting it another way, I was seeking confirmation from the Lord in respect of where I should go? Whilst praying with a church brother, I recall the Divine Spirit leading him to say **"GET YOUR PASSPORT READY, YOU ARE GOING TO TRAVEL"**. My spirit was overwhelmed oddly enough still confused since I wanted to know from God where I was going.

I held on to this prophecy for weeks and weeks never losing focus. Whilst returning from church one day, a still small voice said, **"GO ON A TWENTY-ONE DAY FAST"** which seemed a joke since I am already a slim person and wasn't prepared to lose any more weight. Could I see myself going without food for so long? For weeks I struggled to come to terms with this, then suddenly, something happened! After attending a women's conference, a woman from my church approached me saying **"GIRL I AM GOING TO ENGLAND AND I'M NOT LEAVING YOU BEHIND!"** It was then that the penny dropped.

STARTING TO PACK

After heading home and starting to pack, I informed my landlord of plans to migrate. ***"Carrol you can't leave me, you are a good tenant"***. With comforting tones I assured her my eyes were fixed on leaving Jamaica; there was no going back, so much so, I fasted for about 14 days until severe hunger began to wrack my body insomuch I started negotiating with God: **"JUST THIS ONCE LORD"!** That Sunday, I made shake and baked-chicken with rice-and-peas- and-vegetables. The spirit of greed had taken over and no sooner than I ate the food, I started to vomit so that from that day onward, I refrained from eating until the 21 days were ended. God had engineered a plan and was determined to bring it to pass.

During the fast, I was able to come up with $16,000 paid as a deposit for my air ticket yet the total of $48, 000 was nowhere in sight. Suddenly by the time the fast came to an end, the Lord starts to open up the doors for financial help. My uncle from Canada donated $200 dollars and asked his cousin in England to donate £200, plus my mother's $200 from her job in Grand Cayman, and other monies received, I reached the exact target! Better still, my uncle asked his cousin in England to receive me. My 21-day fast ended with God opening so many doors I was amazed even my mum made an effort to contribute financially! Working in Grand Cayman, seemed her greatest opportunity to get away from dad's oppressive regime enjoying six years whereby she along with my brother made an investment in buying her own house.Sadly this was short lived when she went back home to Jamaica because the woman she was looking after in Grand Cayman died.

ESCAPING FROM THE CHILDREN'S DAD

Roger came out of prison and was now the saving grace to keep the children whilst I secretly prepared to migrate to the UK. During the 21-day fast, the children was with their dad. That was the week before the ninth of April 2000; which was the very day I left Jamaica soil.. With no time to lose, I phoned him in the misery of his ignorance: **"CAN I HAVE THE KIDS FOR THE DAY TO TAKE THEM TO DEVON HOUSE TO BUY ICE CREAM?"** With no hesitation he agreed to send them straight away so we spent a lovely afternoon in town. The whole day seemed like a mystery.

Hours were shifting so fast and I didn't know how best to say good bye: I just kept holding them closer and closer! God knew the pain, the awful pain of separating from my girls. My next door neighbour in whose house I spent the night before leaving Jamaica, had no idea I was migrating, only my friend Cheryl whose house I stayed during the tenure of the 21-day fast. Well-dressed along with the kids heading off with another friend who took the responsibility to take the kids back to their dad. Frankly, I preferred to keep it secret so word didn't reach their father. He had a vengeance for me, worse now he had just got out of prison. All I prayed for, was a safe escape from their dad. As we drove to the airport, I specifically instructed them not to say anything to him when they went back home, but wait until I cleared immigration. Also, wait until I reach my destination before phoning to let them know I had arrived safely.

- Chapter 19 -

LANGUAGE LITANY OF FILTH

Landing in the UK with no money made me utterly dependent on my cousin who came to the airport to fetch me. Upon approching immigration I underwent a series of questons. I was shaking so much but appear to be brave. They seemed intimidating but I manage to keep my calm. It was the good Lord who enabled me to give accurate response. For example:what was the age of one of my cousin son. They put me to sit down for a long time which made me the last person to clear immigration. One of the question was ,what was the age of one of my cousin's children? I answered 9 yeard old. That was the answer that let me through.

On reaching home, she managed to secure a phone card so I could phone the children's father to let him know I was in Britain. Pressure cooker? Put on de pressure!!! When the Mad Shark realised I was 9,000 miles away on British soil, he came down with some of the roughest, some of the hardest...come again... a litany of filth...what a lot of filth! Curse words!!! Pure cursing and swearing!!! This must be hell! Satan in charge: the man gave me such a roasting on the telephone!!! I just smiled and kept my cool... Even if I wanted to say 'naughty boy', I couldn't even get a word in edgeways so I just hung up ('smiles').

ADAPTING TO LIFE IN BRITAIN

England United here I come, it hardly got to two weeks before my cousin was giving me stress. This involved me going to bed on an empty stomach since I was offered no food. She claimed when she goes on holiday she take holiday money with her. Worst came when we stopped speaking altogether and her two sons were rummaging through my suitcase for my passport as their mum suggested she wanted to put me on a plane back to Jamaica. I was too smart for her because I smelled the plan of the wicked witch and decided to sleep with my passport in my bossom (Bust). My other cousin who had given me the £200 to help with my air fare, had made contact. by which time, I was flung outside –suitcase in hand and door slammed in my face. The pillar-box of a phone box was my saving grace. By reversing the call, I was able to tell her where I was, so she could come and rescue me. She came along with a Grand Uncle who welcomed me with open arms so yes, I was offered to sleep on the settee downstairs –he and wife occupying two rooms upstairs.

To me, the culture shock alone was enough. People sounded so different when they spoke. London cockney accent sounded so strange perhaps stranger than the standard English I am accustomed to. Whether it was in the market for fruit and veg, or on a bus, the currency seemed so different from the Jamaican dollars –British pounds as I understand it, is a lot stronger than the Jamaica dollar.

As for the people, it struck me how diverse they were. I felt hopeless at recognising who was Scottish, Irish, Welsh never mind those from far-flung regions within Europe. i.e. Poles, French, Swedes, Germans, Italians and so forth. Amazed by the thought of some Asians or Africans having a background of anything up to four or five languages made me feel like working harder to appreciate the common bond of cultural differences. How beautiful they all looked in national costume not forgetting the whole variety of foods apart from the likes of fish and chips.

I was beginning to feel safe now my Grand Uncle was putting me in touch with family relations I hadn't even heard of. Better still, taking me to South Chelsea College to enrol on a basic computer course along with Maths and English. As my Sponsor providing enough motivation for me to complete the City & Guilds Maths and English also Computer Programming I manage to obtain a certificate. After careful reflection on my achievement at my first college I realised I wasn't satisfied in terms of career choice, so I got enrolled at Bromley College to pursue the Access to Teaching Course. At this stage I realised that I was struggling with tense, and sentence construction. At this stage I was advised by my personal tutor to re-enrol on the Access foundation course which would get me up to the level to manage the Access Course. I took his advice. After one year I obtained the pre- Access Cerificate which allowed me to enrol on the Access to Teaching course. I completed it and obtained my certificate. At this stage my determination had paid off and I was now feeling overjoyed.

My visa application status allowed for a further year extended stay which was great news as I opened my mail first thing in the morning to acknowledge my passport and a covering letter from the Home Office. My Grand Uncle didn't seem too pleased ***"You turn somebody now!"*** as if to say I was outstaying my welcome.

RELATIONS TURNING SOUR

Over a period of time believe it or not, this Grand Uncle of mine, was making inappropriate advances as I slept on the settee at nights. Like Ive said before, one of the bedrooms upstairs was occupied by his wife who suffers from dementia. By rejecting his advances over a period of time, made him increasingly distraught, ill-tempered and bad-mannered. This wasn't helping my cause. Worse when I told him I started working part-time plus embracing the opportunity for another job. With income from both jobs, I started providing my own food.

I was intending on saving enough money to purchase my childrens' air ticket to come and join me. ***"This is not a good idea"*** he remarked ***"for a start, you haven't got any place to accommodate them"***. Actually, he was right on this though he was miserable and spiteful in every other respect. All I required from him was a roof over my head. As tension rose between us, he started keeping a close eye to see if any guys from church were talking to me. For instance, he would get all overly protective which made me feel more pressured and confused.

One day by coincidence while I was out and about, I met one of my friends from Jamaica who had nowhere to live, so I took her to him asking if she could stay with me until she found somewhere to live. Thankfully, he agreed. This was a good way of diverting this monster from bothering me goodness what a relief!

- Chapter 20 -

HALLELUJAH AT LAST AN OPEN DOOR (As well as meeting Val for the first time)

Coming from work one evening and standing at the bus stop I met this guy called ***Val*** *We kept in touch and spoke regularly. One day whilst at home the phone rang, I thought it was Val but it was a cousin I hadn't met.*

"I am only a phone call away" said a warm, comforting telephone voice.

"Who are you?"

"I am your long lost cousin"

"Long lost cousin from where? Where did you get my number from?"

"Your sister gave me" said the solitary tone of a polite male voice.

"I know it's not the best news you want to hear, but my mother has died leaving a five-bedroomed house; as it stands one of my brothers is the sole occupant at the property".

As the conversation progressed, I realised I was faced with an open door, hence a solution to the discomfort and harassment of having to sleep on the downstairs settee of my Grand Uncle's house. With good dreams, no one wants to wake up; to my joy, I could hardly believe the wonderful offer extended to me to move into a house –no rent except a little help with bills which would be required of me. Goodness me, it gets better and better! So I took the offer and moved in.

Standing by my side all this time, was a male friend named **Val** short for **Valentine**. Telling me that he lived as a single man in a one-bedroomed flat –insisting he wanted me to visit and see from the contents of his wardrobe, that there was no woman in his life- in the same breath offering to help me get re-settled in my new five-bedroomed accommodation. No sooner than moving in, I noticed something rather unusual about my wonderful cousin. From what he told me, he paid regular visits to his mum's grave. i.e. every Sunday morning at a specific time. To be honest, I found this too weird.: Going to a graveyard to lay flowers in memory of loved ones, is an acceptable feature of this' society. Frankly, I couldn't understand why he needed to visit every Sunday morning without fail. It seemed there is a hidden agenda.

RUNNING A CHECK ON VAL

Another concern was **Val**: what does he do for a living? According to him, he is a post Graduate within the legal profession so much so, he is up to date with issues regarding immigration and government policy. Currently, he is employed as an Administrator in the Registrar's Office of a University -so he says. I really wanted to check this man out to find out if all he's saying was true? Doubting his sincerity would be difficult if for the most part, he is dressed in suit and tie, well-spoken, well-mannered, sporting an attaché briefcase, always inviting me to restaurants and insisting on paying the bill Still, there are reservations in my mind for instance, it might be useful to ask neighbours living within his own location if they know anything about him.

He introduced me to a female cousin of his living next to his own block of flats telling me he was the one who took her to the UK.. On a one-to-one, I approached her in a friendly manner just to find out if she could tell me anything about him. Seemingly tight-lipped, all she'd say was ***"He was the one who helped me to gain entry to the United Kingdom from Jamaica"*** **"yes but what is he like?"** All she was trying to say basically, is that he is a good person trying to help others end of story. Wasn't long again before I met another cousin of his who was a male, I tried to get information out of him to what sort of person this **Val** was but he was too tight lipped because he was invited from Jamaica by **Val** too. He didn't have much to say other than he was a good person. Seemed like everybody has been rehearsing the same song and got it right. Any way I went with the idea **"He is a good person"**

- Chapter 21 -

CHILDRENS' FARE PAID FROM VAL'S CREDIT CARD

As our relationship plunged to deeper levels, we became intimate. Yes there were those times when I felt weak to the point of abandoning all my reservations: Torn between the love of my daughters in Jamaica, and a man venturing on the threshold of my life at times was too much. Like the pages of an open book, **Val** read my mind day after day and night after night until one day he stopped me in my tracks: **"I WILL GRANT YOU THE DESIRE OF YOUR HEART; DON'T WORRY ABOUT A THING; YOUR CHILDREN WILL BE HERE SOONER THAN YOU THINK"** *"What?"* (Turning my head slowly) **"THEY'RE ONLY A CREDIT CARD AWAY"**, The next day whilst escorting me into town for a meal, he diverted to the nearest travel agent and therewith paid their fare to come to the UK for a holiday. So drawn by his generosity and magnanimous spirit, I must have turned aside in disbelief burying my face in my hands. It took me a while to get over it.

ARRIVAL OF LUCY AND SANDY (not their real names)

With the flight booked and date all set, there was only one week left for my two daughters to materialise from out of my fantasy world to make it through airport controls -then I'd know this whole thing was real and not a figment of my imagination! By way of preparation, I had already furnished a special room with a brand new bed, dressing table and wardrobe. The year was 2001, the month, June and the day, Saturday. With my devoted lover at my side , even though one year in our relationship, I was still restless not knowing whether immigration would have let them through without hassle.

An alarm went off while we were both seated in the waiting gallery of London Heathrow Airport. Everyone was instructed to vacate the area until the place had been thoroughly checked. This was registering a different message. i.e. that God is about to manifest through the storm so His Purpose can be fulfilled. Crowds re-assembled with anticipation as we all encroached on the barrier. From a considerably long way off, all I could see was Lucy running towards my direction with her pullman behind shouting **"MUMMY! MUMMY!! MUMMY!!!"**

FIGHTING BACK THE TEARS (!!!) BY NOW MY TEARS WERE SYNONIMOUS TO GIVING BIRTH TO MY OFFSPRING ALL OVER AGAIN. RIGHT BEHIND WAS SANDY SHOUTING **"MUM"!MUM!!"** WITH A GLINT OF PROMISED LAND WRITTEN ALL OVER HER FACE –THE BROADEST SMILE EVER!!! !!! COMING IN CLOSER PROXIMITY TO MOTHER, BOTH SUDDENLY DISBANDING THEIR TROLLEYS TO RUN INTO MY ARMS. We needed time.yes? Quiet time to bury our faces as we acknowledged a successful rescue-mission from out of a quagmire of separation.

O what a reconciliation! What beauty enthroned in such love! Love is like a bond that can never ever be broken To

God be the Glory; Here we are again; By way of a human instrument chosen for this successful operation, I must accord special thanks to my lover of a man who stood his ground, so much so, he was inspired to finance the air fare of my two daughters. For what has turned out to be the happiest day of my life, I give thanks to both God and man!

- Chapter 22 -

SUDDENLY REALISING I WAS PREGNANT

As the level of intimacy between **Val** and myself became more pronounced, it dawned on me that we were headed in the direction of raising a family. Finding out I was pregnant, added to the confusion of whether he intended to take full responsibility by offering to marry me? With no word from him, this was leading nowhere Within the first week of my children's arrival, the atmosphere was jubilant with celebration: now the whole thing turning into shock because I wanted education -not another child! I had no alternative but to face a further setback of waiting nine months for this child to be born. However I didn't let this divert me from my goal which was to persue education. Although this child was not planned, she might well be a blessing in disguise

On a financial level, things were not exactly easy since I had to be working part-time whilst studying and looking after my two children and pregnant with my third daughter. A year went by; when the child was born, Val decided to name her Weeks following my discharge from hospital I experienced a rush of raw anger compounded by increasing anxiety. I had no idea I was suffering from Post Natal Depression. With mood swings leading further and further into aggression, I started shouting uncontrollably at my two daughters at times even chasing them from one corner of the house to another. I didn't understand what was happening to me. It was later I learnt it was Post Natal Depression.

My little girl's dad was in shock as to why I was behaving so badly. I am not sure he understand what was happening to me. The truth is, I was in shock and my blood pressure was high. With guilt complex, my mood was at its lowest ebb with the prospects of starting work after a six-week stretch; moreover, going back to college three times a week to fulfil my Visa requirements, was too much. God in heaven knows how I was going to cope with all the drama that's been going on in my life.

DRIVEN FROM THE 5-BEDROOMED BY A SUSTAINED DEMONIC ATTACK

Just before I moved out, I had a dream one night as I slept: **"YOU BETTER COME OUT OF MY HOUSE!"** This was the voice of a woman. Not many days later, I went for an afternoon nap and saw myself struggling because someone was attacking me; I was shouting **help! help!! help!!!** My cousin who was living at the house at the time, looked at me and walked away. One morning straight after that, his son came to the door of my bedroom and knocked forcefully: **"YOU BETTER COME OUT OF MY GRANDMOTHER'S ROOM!"**

Under these circumstances I didn't want my kids to become frightened and sick, so I decided to leave. It was at that point that I called a Church sister who was working at a

Women's Refuge 'Eve's Housing For Women'. She decided it would be best if I moved in with my children the same day.

Even though I was not exposed to any physical danger, the fact is, I was psychologically and emotionally traumatised. Now that I needed Val more than ever, he just was not there for me. Not long after moving in the Refuge, we were told we had to leave because of Immigration status. The Social Services re-housed us in Bed & Breakfast facilities only for three days before offering to deport us back to Jamaica. At this appointed time, I had given up studying preferring to go on a desperate search to find somewhere to live. This took another turn as I was asked to leave the premises by the owner. As I packed my belongings and put them outside with the baby in my hand, the Landlord said, ***"Come back inside, I can't let you go outside in the cold with the kids; if it was you alone, I would let you go, but because of the children come back in let us talk".***

- Chapter 23 -

HIDDEN TRUTH OF VAL AT LAST REVEALED

"Who is responsible for these children?" asked the landlord: "Val my baby's dad", I replied.
"Call him!"
"I'll take care of the housing situation" he exclaims on arrival -withdrawing now to speak to me in private.
"I've got something to tell you: there's someone living in the flat –a lady with a baby who got thrown-out of her own flat".
Because he didn't want to come clean on whether the baby was his, I threatened to phone immigration on him. Out of fear he ended-up inviting the children and me to come and stay in the same flat. As soon as the woman in confused state blessed eyes on us, she ran to confer with neighbours next door.

Given that we were crammed for space, it hardly got three weeks before **Val** issued me and my children an ultimatum to find alternative accommodation within two weeks. Throwing us out on the streets in preference to another woman –is what this was about:my daughter is his child and I am her mother? How can he do this to his own flesh and blood?

As the hatred in him grew stronger, I knew I had to face reality. Having the three children especially the one which

was his, made me question his motives in turning us out on to the street –another side of this man; I never realised he was so heartless and cruel. I hadn't got the least idea that he had gone the distance to take me to court to leave the property. One morning I was at the house tidying the baby and the post dropped through the door.
As I opened it I realsied a date was set for a Court hearing. In fact the same morning at 10am. I had less that an hour to get to the court but I managed to quickly dress and leave the baby with the two older ones and rushed to court. The hearing was at Camberwell Crown Court in London. The judge that morning was a God sent. As he listened to my side of story and realised that I had a child for this beast of a man pronounced the following words: **"STAY WHERE YOU ARE, DO NOT MOVE!"**

In defiance of the Court judgment, it wasn't long before he started removing the curtains and changing the locks on the doors, turning-off the electricity and removing the TV from the room while the kids were watching it.It was a good thing I was a sensible woman. When I met Val and we became intimate **SOMETHING SAID TO ME GET HOLD OF EVERY PIECE OF IMPORTANT INFORMATION ABOUT HIM AND WRITE THEM DOWN YOU MAY NOT KNOW WHEN YOU WILL NEED THEM.** I made sure I retained his date of birth, National Insurance Number, full address to the property and energy account number. That was the reason why I could be able to call **British gas** to come and reconnect the electricity. Also the gentleman asked me who I was. I told him I just had a baby for **Val**.

At that time Racquel was only seven months old. Where we lived then was a restless part of Brixton frequented by gangs and drug users.

I'M NOT GIVING UP WITHOUT A FIGHT!

By way of a sudden turn of events, the woman went away for a whole week leaving me with a question: how come she has nowhere to go, yet finding somewhere to stay for a whole week? In protest, I folded-up her bed because we were crammed for space. Val on visiting the flat, questioned my motive for folding up the bed and I told him straight, ***"She won't be coming back; I need the space for my children"!*** This giant-sized woman no sooner he phoned, barged in the flat with a war of words then grabbing me by my hair and flashing me to and fro.. With my two older daughters jumping on her back, I fisted and fisted and fisted to no end!!! By now, the whole thing was blown-up into such a big fight that neighbours next door alerted the Police who came and stopped the fight. After questioning us to who we were I told the officers that **I HAVE A CHILD FOR THE OWNER OF THE FLAT AND THAT HE WAS THE ONE WHO TOOK ME AND MY CHILDREN THERE TO LIVE. WITH FAVOUR ON MY SIDE AGAIN THE WOMAN WAS ORDERD TO LEAVE THE FLAT. She packed and went, I never saw her again..**

WHERE WAS **VAL**? A question to answer. Up to now, I find it hard to believe he was the one who called her to come and attack me then left for her to beat me to a frazzel . Suppose this unknown woman had killed me? Maybe it still wouldn't have mattered. From the earliest of early, I suspected there was another side to him. With men, especially those walking into my life, and lulling me into a false sense of security, I was never wrong about my suspicions.

- Chapter 24 -

THE ONLY THING THAT KEPT ME GOING

Finding somewhere to live was very difficult because my immigration status was still pending. I was visiting one London borough to the other with the hope that a door would open for me to get somewhere to live but nothing; not even an olive branch of an offer! In my spirit a pall of depression was now setting in: at one point, it seemed I had had enough. Were it not for the sake of the children, maybe I would have taken my own life! This was the answer given to the doctor when she asked me to give her one reason why life was worth living when then she diagnosed I was suffering from depression..

Val, the father of my youngest keeping such a low profile didn't help: at a time when most I needed him, he was'nt there. At one point, I remember walking into a church in Camberwell and the preacher exclaiming: ***"Lady at the back, in the name of the Lord stand up: the Holy Spirit has directed me to tell you, that you will be re-housed in a 3-bedroomed accommodation!"***

Through-out the struggle I never forgot that prophecy, that was what keept me through those difficult times.

VAL: THE ULTIMATE BETRAYAL

While **Val** arranged a meeting with the Social Services for me to attend an appointment with them. I thought this would be a breakthrough for me to get somewhere to live. What I didn't know, was that he had a trick up his sleeve. When I went to the meeting that morning, the Social Worker asked me if I knew why I was there. Obviously, I thought my children and I were going to be re-housed. To my ultimate shock and dismay, this was what was said to me: **"I AM GOING TO TELL YOU THE TRUTH: YOUR LITTLE GIRL'S DAD HAD ARRANGED THIS MEETING, FOR US TO TAKE AWAY THE CHILDREN FROM YOU AND DEPORT YOU BACK TO JAMAICA"**.

After I heard these words, I wished the earth could open-up and swallow me. No way was I going to be separated from my children. God's promise, in the face of **Val** and his antics,can never ever be aborted. Not many days hence, as I was envisioned between the early hours of 2:00 and 4:00am, a bright light appeared from out of a wall of darkness followed by the semblance of a white robe. There was no face except for the sound of a voice coming from an image: **"CARROL"**, said the first voice, **"WHY ARE YOU SO AFRAID?"** followed by the voice of a second image, **"CARROL, IF YOU TRUST ME, I WILL BLESS YOU!"**

- Chapter 25 -

NOTTINGHAM HERE I COME!

Whilst going through London's Brookside market (the year was 2003), I stopped to purchase a few items. No sooner than I was about to get on the bus, I heard someone calling me ! This was one of the ladies who prayed me off the night I was about to make my dramatic escape from Jamaica. She was so happy to see me there and then deciding to come home with me. As we talked, she learnt of my difficulties and decided to spend two weeks with me in fasting and prayer.

Throughout the tenure of this time, she shopped to no end, making sure my cupboard and refrigerator were filled with food adding fuel to her motto: 'the Lord is my Shepherd', hence, I should not lack anything'. Like filling me with hope for greener pastures to come, she exclaimed in calm and reflective tones:

" I AM GOING TO NOTTINGHAM AND I AM COMING BACK FOR YOU"

Two weeks later, she returned with a Minister to collect stuffs she had left behind. Strange is it not? When going off to work, I should have left the key under the mat but went to work with it, but this day in question, I took the keys with me purely by accident; God had a plan that day.

Both she and the Minister showed up at my work place. Upon introducing him to me, he exclaimed, **"WHY NOT COME TO NOTTINGHAM?"**. " I don't have any family living there", I replied. **"COME, MY WIFE AND I WILL TAKE CARE OF YOU AND THE CHILDREN"**, he replied. My faith being the person I am, was now activated -telling myself there was no need to doubt the man of God, so I accepted with grace and dignity.
As soon as I got home, the girls were the first to know; thereafter, I bought three suitcases before phoning my friend confirming with her that I have decided on coming to Nottingham. She conveyed to the Minister that I was ready and willing to take the risk. By now I was packed all ready for the move.

No sooner than arriving in Nottingham, God started connecting me with people who were willing to help. Better still, I landed myself a job even before informing those at my work place of change of circumstances. Before I knew where I was, the Minister informed me that he had found rented accommodation for me. The house in question had been locked-up for quite some time, in effect, I was the first to claim tenancy after four years.

Coming from out of the mists of an uncertain world, I was at long last touching base with a cosmos filled with light. Praise God, I was starting to walk with my head held high. trust me I was feeling a fresh veneer of self-confidence. As for the house, three bedrooms it was: weeks on end, I had to come to grips with cleaning and preparation. Then there were schools to sort out for the girls, doctors' appointments as well as college for the pursuance of my own education.

My friend who introduced me to Nottingham, was of enormous help, in fact,becoming even part of my family. She would stay with the kids while I am off to work, mind you, providing for three children and a friend seemed like hard work. However, I didn't complain. The Minister and his wife had been a tower of strength all throughout this time when I was working to make ends meet; hence, I kept telling myself 'look on the bright side'.

Concerning my friend, things were getting to a stage where we both felt uncomfortable so much so, hardly a word exchanged between us; it seemed like the only source of life was the children. Most worrying was the simple fact that she didn't have a job and there was no way of supporting herself because she had immigration difficulties. Things got to a breaking point for her. She was now frustrated of not finding a job in so much that she chose to walk out of the house leaving the children unsupervised. It hurt so much that the only word I could find in the dictionary to describe the moment was "BETRAYAL"!

The real issue of my immigration status started to affect me. For example, Val, my ex was my Sponsor; walking away from him wasn't easy. Now there was a void in my life. Diplomatically, I was in need of a Sponsor; **I MUST MAKE IT CLEAR EVEN-THOUGH I NEEDED SUPPORT FOR SOMEONE TO SPONSOR ME, FINANCIALLY IT WASN'T**

A PROBLEM BECAUSE I WAS WORKING AND COULD SUPPORT MYSELF.

Then again, I was enjoying the challenge of being on my own again but guess what? **Val** started worming his way on the horizon again on the pretext that he needed to make contact with his little daughter; this I wasn't going to refuse because he takes care of his daughter including my other two. He was kind in terms of giving gifts **BUT...HE WANTED TO KNOW WHERE HIS DAUGHTER WAS LIVING, AND I WAS NOT KEEN ON GIVING HIM THAT LEVEL OF INFORMATION.**

I tried various ways for him to stay in contact with his daughter such as taking her to London to see him. On one such occasion, he offered to take us back home. Even now I find it difficult to understand why I couldn't find some kind of excuse to block him. Dropping us home turned out to be deadly. No way could I get rid of this man! Time after time; visiting my turf even without warning:looking straight into my face and telling me he wanted to marry me and be reconciled.

After the saga of living hell he put me through? Manipulating the Social Services to take my children into care whilst ensuring I was deported back to Jamaica in shame and disgrace?

Spewing water out of my mouth seemed like running parallel to his nasty little offer of marriage!The day when his REAL wife showed up from out of the REAL world, she knocked: no sooner had I opened my door she said: **"I'M THE WIFE, I'M THE WIFE"**. Fortunately she opened my eyes. **"I**

KNOW YOU DON'T KNOW WHAT THIS MAN IS LIKE AND HOW DECEIVING HE CAN BE. ALSO, YOU SEEM TO BE A DECENT WOMAN". We chatted at length and a lot was revealed about him; thereafter,I made my decision to break off any type of relationship with him. What's more, I choose to because I didn't want my children to be seeing mixed messages coming from me.

Like a thorn in the flesh, he continued pursuing me; starting now to visit church to convince me he had changed. I wasn't impressed because I hadn't forgotten what he had done to me and my children. With the London years under one-room conditions, he had me embroiled in a nasty dirty fight with an unknown woman and her baby who wanted me out on the streets. For the hell of it, I had no choice but to stand my ground; in the end she had to go. How can I forget?

- Chapter 26 -

SPIRITUAL DISCRIMINATION

My church within the confines of a Nottingham, became a safe haven, until sectors within the Leadership, became aware of links between myself and **Val**. Adding to the complication, was his quest to prove we were family; in other words, this was his scheme he had cooked up to manipulate his way back into my life. Once the church got wind that he was my little girl's father, in their eyes, it seemed clear that marriage was the right and acceptable course to take.

Without knowing the circumstances how far wrong can people be?
In my eyes, they had not even began to scratch at the surface, leaving no less a plethora of unanswered questions: All they saw, was a well-spoken man dressed in a decent suit; Each individual's life is like a book unopened how can you judge a book by its cover? How can they point a finger of censorship at me on the basis of my apparent refusal to marry a man with a chequered history of lies and deceit?

Again, it stands to reason that '*wives*, be submissive to your *husbands*' holds no meaning for me if all my male relationships are chequered with a catalogue of domestic violence and carnal abuse. By marrying this man I would be incurring further hell and destruction, on my life is that what they want? How can the Church preach "*Wives be submissive to your husbands*" to rail road me into blind acceptance just because it says so in the book? To maintain my own safety in the long run, I'd be better-off packing my bag and...wait for it...get the hell out of it!!!

Within my mind I was forming a concept of spiritual discrimination. Was it just my imagination? I heard a voice saying **'WHAT YOU ARE GOING THROUGH IS SPIRITUAL DISCRIMINATION'!** As a woman supposedly 'living in sin' , I was beginning to understand what it felt like to be labelled' an outcast'? What of the Ministerial Team? What was their view on this? Better still, how does God see me?

One Sunday morning I was in church feeling distressed and perplexed and decided to go outside and sit down. Then a woman, a stranger from nowhere appeared saying to me 'God sent me to you', she went on: **"You have two big daughters, one dark one and a chubby brown one"**. My mind went on Lucy; I didn't bother to question her any further. **"God said to tell you He loves you;"** adding more to my baffled expression she asked, **"Do you drive?" " Yes"** I replied.**"Follow me"**; She went outside, then opened a car boot filled with groceries for me and my children.

Oddly enough, this was the very Sunday I was in church enduring torment, more like the tortures of the dammed, every Sunday it seemed worse; no rest for the wicked; Like a miracle from out of nowhere, this woman showed-up believe it or not, I never saw her again until one day whilst shopping at Asda in Hyson Green, I saw a woman reminding me of her. “Shhhh”, she silently replied as I walked across to greet her. *“Are you the lady that came to......that Sunday morning?”* **“Don’t mention it”**, as if playing it down **“It’s God”**; He knows the situation; He knows how best to meet your need.

In another instance not far removed from my own, I remember being in church one Sunday morning when a woman storm-tossed, way-worn, heavy-laden and sad, walked into the very same church. As she attempted to voice her own need, she was abruptly stopped! Making matters worse, the Presiding Minister ordered forthwith that she be put outside. This begs the question: where is compassion in all of this? How would Jesus Christ have dealt with this? For all I care, she may have been disturbing the service -would Jesus have ordered her to be put outside? That is the question I wish to leave with my readers

If nothing, this clearly, is an act of spiritual discrimination. Christ, in a sense, came not to call the righteous. Those who are whole, needing not a physician, only those who are storm-tossed, way-worn, heavy-laden and sad. Where do I stand in all of this? At this particular appointed time of my life I am a compassionate person primarily because of what I have gone through myself. Written on the table of my heart, if I saw a brother/or sister overtaken with a fault, I should endeavour to restore him or her in brotherly albeit sisterly love , so saith the scriptures.

- Chapter 27 -

HERE COMES 'SWEET MAN TULIP' (Is this a trap?)

One particular Sunday after church, I got talking to a young man, one of the regulars sitting mostly at the back row. Hailing from the exotic Jamaican landscape like me; resident on the same housing estate as me. ('trouble??') Seemingly, in his late 30's, charming enough, radiating a facial countenance all too appealing. Homeward bound more often than not, he would offer me a lift since we were headed in the same direction. Sitting in the front seat of his car seemed ever so comforting! Gospel music CDs appeared to be a passion of his; as one is finished, a next and a next and so forth; playing them right the way through till he dropped me at my door. Each car journey becoming all the more relaxing as we shared stories about life in Jamaica. At times he made me laugh so much.

"What's your name? *"Sweet Man but dem call me Tulip!"* **"What is the name on your birth certificate? Can't be 'Sweet Man' can it?** What is your real name?" We laughed it off.

Next, he wanted to know where I was working? Once I told him, he was willing and ready to wait for me then drive me all the way to and back. In the face of such generosity, it seemed so much easier for him to visit me as and when he wanted. Occasionally, he would be invited to share my

Sunday dinner. Before we knew where we were, he would be turning up at times when he wasn't even invited. This made me somewhat uncomfortable so much so at times I didn't quite know how to handle it.
Times and again when he out-stayed his welcome, I was left wondering when am I going to be free to cook my children's dinner, read with them and find out what's been happening at school? Day after day: not even a single day to myself; mostly coming to the house when he knew they were at school. At one point I couldn't stand it any longer: how do I let him know I need breathing space? I had to write a strong letter expressing concerns over his over-familiarity. This left me wondering if this whole thing was nothing but another trap -all too familiar with the men in my life? A trap to drag me down and down into a cesspool of shame and disgrace?

Yet deep deep down I was glad for the company. The trouble with 'Sweet Man Tulip' -or whatever his name is - he came with a mischievous smirk on his face which confused me. This man, friend or foe, might even turn out to be a Protector from my worst fears. Right now, **Val**, my baby girl's father, poses an embarrassment more like Problem Number One so if worse comes to worse, Sweet Man Tulip might be able to stand in the gap and protect me from his relentless advances to worm his way back into my life.

Emotionally and spiritually, I tend to be weak when it comes to standing up to men who are trying to get the better of me. Whilst entertaining the view that 'Sweet Man

Tulip' might be a deadly trap, I had no strategy in place for pushing him off me except allowing him free reign to walk all over my house, sit in my settee, eat my food, laugh as loudly as he wanted – writing him a letter to try stopping him seemed like a waste of time.

PREGNANT AGAIN

Things came to a head when for a special church service one Sunday, he escorted me and my little girl to Birmingham in his car. We ended up coming back to Nottingham rather late that night. with the children deciding to stay on at a friend, he escorted me to my gate; once he got out of the car, he followed me inside carrying one of the bags. We had something to eat followed by a long chat as the night wore on. That night more than ever, I needed the will to stand clear, and point him to the door: **"GET THE HELL OUT OF HERE!"** Oddly enough I couldn't find the gall to tell him, given this was well past midnight.. To this day, I'm left wondering why?

Within days, -O God - I came to the realisation that I was pregnant -no that can't be right: **P-R-E-G-N-A-N-T???** As days and nights followed in solitude and disbelief, I was still asking **"Why? Why now?"** As if chastising myself; **WAIT TILL THE CHURCH HEARS THIS!!!** Already I am 'an outcast' in their eyes, O my God what am I going to do? All such thoughts were now resolved in a desire to have an abortion. Having gone to the clinic, the nurse strongly advised me against it especially with my blood pressure being so high **"IT IS DANGEROUS TO GO DOWN THAT**

ROAD; YOU MIGHT DIE, she warned, so I heeded her advice by going through with the pregnancy. As weeks turned into months, my self-confidence dropped to a low ebb; to make it worse, I avoided going to church.

With all the frustration and confusion going on in my mind, I realised that childbirth was drawing near, hence my admittance to hospital meant I had to await the ultra sound determine the sex of the child. During the ensuing moments, I fell asleep. In my dream, an Indian man came into the Labour Ward holding a baby boy: **"MOTHER, THIS IS NOT AN ORDINARY CHILD"**
-more like a vision in my estimation. The actual result of the ultra sound agreed with the vision O my God I was so overjoyed on realising I took the advice of the nurse by not going through with the abortion:

Sweet Man Tulip was with me from my admittance to the Labour Ward through to the birth of our son (who incidentally, was born on 04/04/05) a healthy baby boy who weighed 6lbs 10 ozs and was he a bundle of joy? Surely enough he was; the spitting image of his father who in effect was present not only at the birth but at the registration. The irony in all this, is that his support was neither material nor financial: not a penny to buy booties for his little feet never mind pampers or milk. The baby I very nearly aborted, was turning out to be the emblem of a treasured friend, I started calling him Jeoffery not his real name Jeoffery didn't even creep. He walked straight away. His progress was rapid in so much by the age of six months, he was laughing (with no teeth?); by the age of one, he was starting to talk. Unlike most babies, he didn't stand around and wait; he was a 'do-it-now' baby.

Given that my relations with the church was not at its best, I still wanted him blessed, so a request for an appointment was made. I liaised with his God Mother who arranged a special white suit to be transported from America.

The day of the baby's blessing arrived with a telephone call from Church Office to report a cancellation. Church politics? With the whole thing sounding like snakes crawling from out of the cupboard, I turned my attention to the good grace of a young Pastor popularly known as Reverend Denval Mc Kenzie which was just as well! This wonderful Minister showed such love and understanding: bringing healing in my moment of despair by inviting me to his church, so I went to have my baby blessed; thank God as one door is closed, another is opened!

TROUBLE AHEAD

The friendship between myself and 'Sweet Man Tulip' got to a stage where I practically became reliant on his good graces to stand as a bulwark of defence against **Val** whose sole intention was to get back into my life. Once, baby Jeoffery 'play-boy' of a daddy realised I was pregnant, his level of enthusiasm became less, his personality changing to the point of little or no response even in my own dilemma over the issue of abortion. Hardly bothering to come to the house as joyous and enthusiastic as he used to. At the end of the day, perhaps he saw me as a cosmetic plaything only for the purposes of lust and adventure??

With **Val** my little girl's dad, there was no letting-up: liaising with the church as much as he could, so he could put pressure on me to marry him. What I couldn't understand was why would he be putting pressure on me for a reconciliation after his long list of betrayals for God's sake this is a married man! What's more, I had checked him out: He's got a criminal past yeah yeah he's been to prison for bashing women; has the church ran a CRB Police check on him? Talking of CRB, I am checked every six months; till now there are no skeletons in my cupboard; on that score, I have got nothing to hide.
In the face of all this there were fears around immigration and Sponsorship. Given that my little girl's dad acted as my Sponsor and such sponsorship had now expired, I needed it renewed but dared not ask him for fear he seized the opportunity to make my life a misery. Already, he was making special journeys from London to come and watch to see if I was in a relationship with my son's dad? Where was 'Sweet Man Tulip' in all of this? I doubt if he was of any help: for a start, nobody seemed to know his real name. Again: was he in a position to stand sponsorship for me?
I felt pressured and confused, wanting to relate the whole situation to the Pastor of my church but dared not. Given that my level of mis-trust was of such, I was now feeling unworthy and ashamed.

My baby girl's dad started making plans for us to get married and that he was going to buy a house. Pleading and pleading with me to come to have a look, so I went purely out of curiosity. To be honest, I knew he was as broke as the day I met him. I think he was doing it just to impress me. The house fell through; it didn't surprise me in the least. So cunning and deceiving, he wouldn't rest: now he started lavishing finances not only on his daughter but on my two other girls -stopping at nothing to impress me. This made me all the more determined not to have anything to do with him.

This particular Friday no sooner had he travelled from London and saw me and my son's dad talking, he was so upset that he drew a machete to start chopping him up. Walking off in a huff, he thought of an even better idea. i.e. taking the ruthless step of trying to disgrace me in the church of which I was well-known. He wrote to the Pastor telling him how much he had secured a mortgage for a house for us to live together; he claimed I rejected his offer, me preferring to live a life of sin. How manipulating and controlling can one get?
In truth, I was doing my best to keep a safe distance; no way was I going to be rail roaded or cajoled into his best laid plans, in fact I am glad his housing plans came to nought. Leaving me stronger and more determined than I had ever been. This time more than ever, I was not going to allow myself to be controlled or manipulated by anyone. Registering my message loud and clear, nothing was going to shift or move me. Had he succeeded in obtaining his so-called mortgage, both me and my children would be uprooted and planted on his own turf so as to allow him to perpetuate his shabby old tricks year-in-year-out.

One night no sooner had I retired to bed, I dreamt he was holding his little girl in his arms beaconing with his other hand: **"Carrol come over to me"**, and was stretching at me. As I stretched to touch him, a Voice said **"Look down!"** All I saw was a **A DITCH** I mean a deep **DITCH** between us. I replied saying **"I can't because if I come over to you, I will fall into the ditch"**, and that's when I awoke from my sleep.
Not many days later,two women came to pray with me. Sadly one of them passed away a few years ago. I must give thanks for the fact that they brought clarity to my dream; incidentally, I listened in humility. On the said day as they were praying, they suddenly switched into unknown tongues then switching back into English: **"Pharaoh, Pharaoh, let my people go!"**

Hence, the final straw that broke the camel's back: this was where I found the final burst of energy to break away from this God-forsaken relationship. From that day onward, it was as though we parted company for good physically. Till now, there has been no further communication except for the phone lines -incidentally, he is currently residing abroad. Finally, there is a reason for everything. I dare not say any more on this matter!

- Chapter 28 -

TULIP's DOUBLE LIFE UNMASKED!

Tulip, as I was saying, was present at the birth of our son Jeoffery. It was good he decided to present himself, but I didn't know there was another side to him –this was soon to be found out big time! Abraham Lincoln named amongst the Founding Fathers of the American constitution once said: ***"you can fool some of the people some of the time, but you can't fool all of the people all of the time!"*** Nobody can preach like Mr Sweet Man 'Tulip'. Church is his middle-name; in effect taking every opportunity to preach the devil off his throne. This man could fool Abraham Lincoln never mind the devil himself. Christ and Him crucified and all that goes with it: yet for all of this, there is one thing he never told me, sadly enough, I had to find out for myself:

According to plan, he was supposed to come to my house one morning to help with some painting. When I saw time was going and no sign of him, it came to me that perhaps I could venture into the lonesome bachelor flat of his just to hurry him on. Good I've got strong nerves as I knocked on his door only to be met by a woman. Calling him by another name, she shouted ***"there's somebody to see you!"*** His eyes suddenly bulged as he glimpsed me from a distance. Coming to his senses, he greeted me in subdued tones –a kind of nervous tremor followed by a forced smile –are you o'right? A confident man now looking like a frightened child (good and proper…) All I said to him as I walked away was, ***"don't worry!"*** Not much longer after this drama unfolded, I realised he was living with a woman who in effect gave birth to his child some two months after the birth of Jeoffery. Not much long after, disaster suddenly struck in his life: I heard that his motor vehicle was burnt and his house was set on fire!

One day whilst at college, I was faced with yet another shock when I came home later that day to find a note with crime number posted through my letter-box by Police insisting that I report to the Station immediately to answer accusations from Mr Sweet Man 'Tulip' that I was the one who burnt his van and set his house on fire –talk about wickedness and betrayal??? This is a pattern; trust me it happens in every single relationship I have ever formed with a man. All of these men oddly enough with staunch affiliations with church can you believe? Backsliders?? My message is simple: Christians, be on your guard and don't be fooled. What has happened to me can happen to anyone.

On arrival at the Station, I was asked to identify my whereabouts within the time-stretch of these criminal activities. At the said time, I was at Peoples' College pursuing the QAA Diploma in Health and Social Care. There and then, I sought leave to produce written verification from my Tutors to say I was in class. Subsequent to this, the Officers had to go back to the drawing board to locate who they were looking for. Let me get back to Jeoffery, my baby boy and all of the antics of his father: for instance, the name he registered his son in is patterson "" whilst operating under a different name. This was now becoming a source of worry; for instance, why is he shifting from name to name like somebody trying to run away from something?

In the spate of confusion, I sought advice from the Registrar of births. Sweet Man 'Tulip' was the name Jeoffery's father gave me on the day I first met him. When I pressed him for verification of his name, we both laughed it off. The Registrar advised me not to make too much of an issue over a name. Instead, I should name my child in accord with my own good will and pleasure –so I just left it at Jeoffery Patterson!

Not long after, I heard through the grapevine, that this very same Mr Sweet Man 'Tulip' was cornered by a squadron of Police vans and cars, taken into custody and charged with fraud. This meant going to court and sent down. If my information is correct, he was held on remand in H.M. Nottingham Prison before sent on to H.M. Leicester Prison to serve his sentence. When I heard all these things, I thought to myself "what goes round, comes round"! During this cycle of harassment, confusion and lies, I still went on to gain my QAA qualification thanks to the powers that be!

- Chapter 29 -

INKLINGS OF BETRAYAL WITHIN THE HOME

My daughters no more little girls were blossoming into teen adults as they gravitated to their own social circles within the ranks of the church.

At the backdrop of all this, an overseas telephone relationship was now developing between my elder daughter and the demon behaving father back there in Jamaica who would stop at nothing to glean as much information as he could of our lives and how we were living it.

This selfsame wretched of a man, noted for harassing both me and my 15-year-old sister from all those years ago, was now holding sway over both my daughters. Given that they were showing signs of rebelliousness, I took a moment or two to counsel my elder daughter: "You think I haven't told the Pastor everything that goes on in this house?" –huffing and puffing. Hell on earth I couldn't believe what I was hearing!

These children are my family and family should respect confidentiality and stand together no matter what. What happens within the confines of our own home is if no concern to outsiders. I am not saying I was the most perfect mother but **I FIGHT FOR MY CHILDREN**: Even now as I speak, there is a letter amongst my belongings where my older daughter told me how much their father had been neglecting them while they were back there in

Jamaica. I am not under any compulsion to prove evidence of commitment in respect of my role as a parent.

I LOVE MY CHILDREN; I KNOW I LOVE THEM BECAUSE I CHOOSE TO TAKE THEM TO THE UK AFTER ALL I'VE BEEN THROUGH WITH THEIR DAD. ANY SENSIBLE READER VENTURING THROUGH THESE PAGES, WILL APPRECIATE THE HELL I WENT THROUGH TO WRENCH THEM FROM A LIFE OF TORMENT AND YOU TELL ME THIS ISN'T LOVE?

MY FIFTEEN-YEAR-OLD OF A YOUNGER DAUGHTER

During the time I was experiencing all kinds of stress with the likes of Mr Sweet Man 'Tulip', my fifteen-year-old started to give me no end of grief. She was staying out late with girls from our church; lingering in the neighbourhood and in town. With her behaviour becoming increasingly difficult, it became clear she was influenced by others within her circle. She would leave for church and never return home. For the likes of her rebellion and bad behaviour. For example one day she asked to go somewhere providing that the chores given were accomplished, which weren't: **"You are not going out today". Her response was " You think I don't know how to use my mouth? I can let Social Services take away the two little ones from you".** I remember on one particular occasion, she left for a Tuesday Evening Bible study, and was taken to her friend's home by the Pastor of the Church can you imagine? Without even as much as a phone or text message to let me know where she was? Leaving me worried throughout the night unable to sleep?

The following morning, school phoned and I wasn't able to give an account of my child because of some irresponsible person who claimed he/or she was doing the right thing? No communication with me from church level is like pouring salt into the wound? What right have they to manipulate my parental rights like this? I have never told any church member that my children were hungry and in need of help, nor have I ever sought their material or financial involvement on any aspect of my life?

One morning whilst at home, I sought to discipline her on grounds of disobedience: as I stepped towards her, she ran into the airing cupboard, phoned her best friend who in turn rang the Pastor so a whole gang of them was monitoring my home life. In turn bringing me to the brink of pursuing Legal Action to protect the privacy of my home. Why was this happening? Phoning church Headquarters to engage them in what was happening but they weren't interested? Not even to call a meeting to discuss instabilities in relation to my daughter?
At one point she got into trouble at school with the said girl. i.e. her best friend according to her? Money was taken from a Teacher's handbag and I had to repay the £25 since the money was shared between them both. Warning my daughter against whom she chose as friends was like pouring water over a duck's back. Paying no attention to my admonitions.

Running away from home at the age of fifteen, provided even more torment; this time she wasn't answering her phone. It took the Social Services to locate her at the house of a church lady who bore a grudge against me so much so when I went to the house to make inquiries, she told me my daughter wasn't there. I went home then returned the same night: "where is my child?" "No sign of her she must be at church", she replied.

By the time I drove my car to the church only to realise she was parked outside hmm that's suspicious! Asking for the whereabouts of my daughter was a waste of time except for a wall of silence from all who were gathered inside, so I went back outside challenging her: "My daughter is a minor; she is under age; Is she living here or not, I want to know. If in fact, she is living on your premises, how come you are telling me she is not there?" In slimy underhand tones: **"Not because you are her mother, that doesn't give you the right to her!** (huffing and puffing)!
The following Monday morning I was at home getting the children ready for school when the door knocked: it was two female Police Officers. **"Are you Mrs Carrol O?"** I was married then. "Yes", I replied. "You assaulted one Mrs ...... and we are here to arrest you". Flushed with disbelief: **"I am looking after my children to take to school, so I'll come when I find time". "When will this be?" "Wednesday"**, On Wednesday evening of my arrival, they put me in a cell. In little or no time, I was escorted to another room to be finger-printed and a swab was taken.

Whilst in the Interview Room, these were the words of the Officer: "We have had a report from the Pastor of a church to the effect that you dragged Mrs from her car then started beating her in her head; she was beaten severely." Opting now for the opportunity to invite a criminal Lawyer though proceeding nonetheless with a first draft of the interview. All I was seeing in my mind's eye was the cunning and craftiness of a full-scale conspiracy egged-on by my daughter.

On realising my child had left home with no information as to where she was living, I informed the Social Services who in turn donated information to update me on the actual address where she was living. This meant the woman was now communicating with the Benefits Child Support Agency with a view to taking ownership and responsibility thereby posing as my child's guardian. Based on a dream I had, I woke up with an impression that she turned my daughter out of the house. In reality, my daughter confessed that she had actually been thrown out of the house with no access to any of these monies. That is why she wanted to leave so yes, I was absolutely right to drive my car to this woman's house to find out what the hell's going on!

What shocked and confused me most, is the extent to which the Pastor was prepared to stand and support a woman to go behind my back and steal parental rights to my child? Even to the extremes of concocting a story about me dragging the said woman from her car and beating her mercilessly?

In the mean time whilst pursuing this matter, another Court Case believe it or not, was planned by sectors within the Church to effect child abuse charges against me. My two daughters in full support were, supposed to be victims. In my absence, The Social Services informed me of remarks made by the Judge:

“These daughters seem very well cared for. Cases of abuse, do not normally reflect children looking as well-adjusted as these!”

“SUBSEQUENT TO THIS COURT HEARING, THE SOCIAL SERVICES CARRIED OUT THEIR OWN INTERNAL INVESTIGATION ONLY TO FIND OUT THAT THE CHURCH WAS DIRECTLY RESPONSIBLE FOR BRINGING COURT ACTION, HENCE AN IMPASSIONED PLEA WAS MADE TO MY 15-YEAR-OLD “GO BACK HOME TO YOUR MOTHER!”

In relation to the other Court Case in which I was supposed to have dragged a woman from her car and battered her in her head, my Defence Team (Cartwright and King), exposed the criminal history of the said woman in Court thereby stating that she had previously done five years in prison for drug dealing, charged in another for perverting the course of justice, charged in yet another for stealing cars. My Solicitor went on to assure the Court that the whole saga was orchestrated by sectors within the Church with full backing from a Pastor who was prepared to concoct nothing short of **a bag of lies**. (Shame!!!) The Prosecution case didn't stand a chance why? The Judge saw through a quagmire of cheap little gone-past-sell-by-date tactics that didn't work: for instance, **THE WOMAN DIS- RESPECTING MY AUTHORITY OVER MY CHILD, STORMED OUT OF COURT!!!** She literally ran away…**"THANK YOU JESUS"**, (whispering to myself) **"NO WEAPON FORMED AGAINST ME SHALL PROSPER!!!"**

Prophecy: WICKEDNESS ENTERED THE GIRLS HEART AGAINST ME.

In the light of all the confusion and frustration coming from the children and the church, I decided to visit a completely different environment. i.e. a local church in my community where the Pastor is a white man. After the sermon, he was calling for people to come to the alter for prayer. Upon reaching the alter, he spoke to me directly saying: "WICKEDNESS HAVE ENTERED YOUR CHILDREN'S HEART AGAINST YOU!"

Could this be because the church has had a bad influence on my children or, could it be that the demon from their father which previously had bad influence on my sister now re-visiting my children to turn their hearts against me?

- Chapter 30 -

THE STRAW THAT BROKE THE CAMEL'S BACK

A really sad breakdown of communication between my eldest daughter and me, came at a time when I could have done with some help from her.
A hard kernel to crack, was that pertaining to my two younger siblings who at that time were in the nursery and needed to be collected before closing time at 6:00pm each week day. With my regular work shifts finishing at 8:30pm, how was I going to do this?

All this coincided with my daughter's studies at Nottingham Trent University. Easily enough, something could have been worked out in relation to her free evenings? "Why don't you ask your friend from up the road?" 'My friend from up the road', like pouring salt into the wound was the principal architect responsible for the break-up of my short-lived marriage let's not go into that...

After explaining certain difficulties with my works Manager, we agreed my 1-hour break could be re-scheduled as near enough to 6:00pm so as to allow me sufficient time to collect my children from the nursery then on to a friend's, so I could be back at work by 7:00pm. This whole thing believe it or not, was hanging like a tenuous thread that might break at any moment. Pressure was building up amongst the girls working alongside me **"Why is she afforded special privileges to come and go as she pleases?"**

My blood pressure was beginning to rise as nervous exhaustion began taking its toll –and the bottom line –I had no option but to give up the job for the sake of my own sanity. This whole saga, seemed like bad timing especially in the wake of the unfortunate break-up of my marriage no use crying over spilt milk! Had things been different, my partner in terms of Mr O, would have been the ideal person to assist in combining our responsibilities so I could still be able to hang on to my job; nevertheless, it wasn't to be.

MARRIAGE SHORTLIVED

For the likes of a marriage that lasted only two years, what did I see in this man? Putting it another way what did he see in me? On a hazy afternoon, I had just finished my shopping and walking out of Tesco when I practically stumbled into this man eyeing me like a hawk from head to foot: "What are you staring at? (entering the supermarket with a woman by his side) **"Don't you have a woman walking with?" "I am not his woman", she replied "He is looking for a woman to form a relationship with"..**

Talking about tall, dark and handsome, for a moment he sported the template of a romantic figure. What's more, he was soft spoken and his eyes looked as wily as a fox. Another weakness of mine with men sad to say, I can be easily distracted when not focussing on energies to do with my own spiritual progress. There is an old maxim that says, not all that glitters is gold. As a matter a fact the devil knows what all of us need. At that moment I was going through Immigration problem and just needed a break.

Luckily this relationship never break me enough to send me to mental institution..

I had no idea the day would come when I was in a spot of bother and needed his help. Whilst at home, I needed my car to go out one afternoon but couldn't because one of the tyres was flat and surely enough I called on him. Within minutes he turned up to take away the burst tyre and bring back a new one. This turned out to be the one significant factor that brought us together with the whole thing happening so fast. To be truthful, I really was impressed that day so much so he seemed like a God-send! How could this man be a God-send and he wasn't even a Christian so yes, this was bringing me into conflict with church and Bible- based teachings to do with being unequally yoked with unbelievers. Another situation militating against our relationship was that to do with my elder daughters –they didn't take kindly to him. A mere mention of marriage –hence my new name Mrs O –drove them away! The straw that broke the camel's back, was when I expressed an invitation to move into Mr O's house once we got married –provoking new waves of rebelliousness!

Why weren't my daughters happy for me? Why couldn't they find it in their hearts to wish me well? Great things come in small parcels so much so I felt really honoured when they chose to turn up to the wedding! Now as I put pen to paper, it is possible they may have seen something I didn't. For all I care, they may have been trying to say "look mum, this man is not right for you; there is something in

the atmosphere that doesn't add up you being a church woman for a start"
Even on the very day of marriage as my elder daughter stood up to give a speech, she made it clear she hadn't got anything to say!

Weeks turned into months as I began to honour the suspicions of my two daughters: Increasingly I became weighed-down and suppressed by a male partner who had no respect for God nor man. Each time I felt the urge to pray, hence inviting him to join me "you pray", was his response. "I can pray for myself"; sharing my life with this man was tantamount to casting pearls before swine.

On the economic horizon the biggest problem for him, was keeping up with mortgage payments for his house which was becoming increasingly dilapidated. i.e. in Grantham. Given that his earning power from week to week was just a drop in the ocean, I suggested we move to my three bedroomed in Radford and rent out his house instead. He agreed; once we moved in, we took out a joint bank account whilst entering his name on the tenancy agreement of my house in Radford. All this was short-lived: two sets of tenants occupied the premises which he owned and wasn't paying the Mortgage and the level of dilapidation was so bad that the Mortgage company had no choice but to re-possess the house! One set of tenants can you imagine, wasn't even paying any rent so yes, this was a big loss for Mr O and his ambitions.

In spite of all this, I was willing to give this marriage a chance given that my Immigration status was a factor yet to be resolved by the Home Office. That wasn't the only factor; I married him because I loved him. Unfortunately Home office decided not to sort me out in my married name but in my previous name I enterd the country in "Miller". During the time Mr O made an application for updating the visa to my current married name then . His request was turned down on the basis of special favour on me as the letter from Home Office allowed me the right to live and work in the UK. Enabling me therefore, to look after my children. In the eyes of the Home Office, I assumed, his position was weak financially! The fact that our marriage was on its way out, would have been a bad time for him to be allocated a Spouse Visa to exercise control over my life thereby working against me to have both me and my children deported back to Jamaica!

December 2010 saw the ending of a tragic two years living with this man. During September 2011 whilst away on a short visit to Jamaica, I ensured my house was lock-alarm-fitted thereby arranging with neighbours to keep watch. And yes, it was burgled, and ramsacked; thankfully a neighbour saw him leaving the property and phoned the person left in care of the property; this was his best man during our wedding, this could be seen as a good idea? I keep asking myself. This could seen as a conspiracy between them. I didn't know about this until I stepped back on the shores of the Uk. Whilst driving home, the friend said to me **"Something happened whilst you were away" I didn't want to disturb your holiday so I decided to wait until**

you get back to tell you". My heart skipped a beat. "Mr O broke into the house", said the friend. According to him, this shows how low in morals Mr O was. Could this be a conspiracy between them two? Police were called and he was arrested in the face of strenuous denials from him. His words: **"I hate you because you make Police arrest me!"** Also, according to the Police he was not able to reveal the outcome of the case: this goes to show how low a man would want to go to destroy a woman.

Another sad factor leading to the break-up of my marriage was much to do with a relationship blossoming between himself and a woman further up the same street where we lived. Day after day, she would be coming to hang out with him whether I was at home or not. Not to mention one Sunday I was at church, and I came back home to find her in my house. "What are you doing in my house?" ***"Your husband left me to finish cook your dinner because he has to take Mr Walker to dominoes"..***

No sooner than a break up between my ex- and I , she stopped coming to the house except for an occasion when she knocked on my door to push letters of disgust and trying to undermine me, when in fact she is the one who should feel bad, because she wouldn't leave my marriage alone. When she couldn't find anything to discredit me; she and my ex- planned a wicked act on me by claiming that she lent me £100. She lent it to him the same year when they went Christmas shopping in Birmingham.

When he walked out of the marriage, she was unable to get back her money from him. She came to me and request his mobile number, I asked her why she wanted it. According to her she was going to ask him to pay back the money he borrowed. He refused so I became the scape goat. Within months I was issued with a summons to go to Court to answer charges against a background that she loaned me money which I didn't return? The Judge in throwing the case out, asked why was it that she had to wait until my marriage was wrecked before trumping-up such a malicious charge? The case was dismissed by exclaiming the following words : **"EVEN IF YOU CHOOSE TO APPEAL I WILL NOT ACCEPT".** With that; she left with her head hanging down. Again I maintain that **No weapon formed against me shall prosper!**

- Chapter 31 -

SABOTAGE: 1, 2, 3 and 4

SABOTAGE: HIGHER EDUCATION – throwing the towel in??

Whilst the swing doors of Higher Educational opportunities are open to those fulfilling the necessary criteria, I might well consider myself blessed in the sense that on no less than three occasions, I have been invited to embark on the journey that leads to Degree status. Faced with a myriad of opportunities on no less than three occasions, yet not even as much as a foot in the door? Some might dismiss this as pure idle talk yet it's true.

Let's take Nottingham University's Medical School for Nursing and Midwifery: what gave me the impetus to apply for study, was more to do with groundwork already covered at Peoples' College in the wake of having gained the QAA Diploma in Health and Social Care, hence, it was time for me to pursue a Degree. Because my passport had less than three months left before expiry date, I was refused admission on the grounds that my interviewers didn't know if Home Office was going to extend my visa –sounds plausible enough!

Take another example: I now approached Nottingham Trent University with a view to embarking on a Degree

Course given that my dream in life is to qualify either in Nursing or Social Work. Again, I was told I would be seriously considered on the recommendation of following a Learn Direct course in English so I did exactly as required with the dismay of failing on each occasion so yes, in the end I gave up with premonitions that something wasn't quite right?
Forces working against me call it what you will: my qualification in GCSE English was part of the paperwork produced during the course of this interview so why has English become the principal determinant all of a sudden? I started to think somewhere along the line, somebody must be setting me up to fail? After putting all my irons in the fire, it looked as though I was left only to walk away with nothing, so much so I turned my attention to Derby University application system.

Two attempts were made to send my information through to the administration desk but they got lost in transit. After having a talk with the Course Tutor, I was advised to give the documents to an African friend of mine who studied there. The same evening not long after deciding to bring the paperwork, I knocked on his door but he wouldn't answer –oddly enough, there was light in the house as well as considerable movement. Knocking on his door adding to my dismay, was just a waste of time so I went back home and phoned the Course Tutor who suggested I bring my papers myself!

The interview went so well in so much I felt relieved; at the end all I was asked to do, was send passport and other documents within a week. No sooner had I ventured from the building on to the car park my African friend popped up out of nowhere: *"What are you doing here?"* I asked. Believe it or not, the man, staring at me, transformed into vapour. Dissolving into nothingness just like a ghostly figure. Calling his name loudly whilst shaking my head leaving me in shock; surely this must be what they call an *out-of-body experience??*

Not long after this episode I was headed towards City Hospital to attend to my son: after parking my car, I heard someone shout "Carrol!" this time for real, it was the same guy. We chatted briefly and he disclosed his disappointment at not finishing the course because they failed him. Mind you, I felt pity for him although to a greater extent preoccupied with the question *–what is the definition of a friend?*

My quest to gain entrance to the course at Derby University was hinged on a reference from Peoples' College without it I am doomed. **"IF YOU ARE EXPECTING THE HEAD OF DEPARTMENT TO GIVE YOU A REFERENCE, YOU ARE WASTING YOUR TIME"**, said someone from the Office on the telephone. **"SHE IS GOING TO GIVE YOU A BAD REFERENCE"** "Why" I asked **"BECAUSE YOU'RE TOO MUCH OF A CHRISTIAN"**. That is to say, all of my efforts to get into higher education led nowhere –the whole thing amounting to nothing but the subject of sabotage.

SABOTAGE: failure to address my child's educational needs

One school assured me that assessment data in regards to my 12-year-old child's report would be sent to her new school. This was done; Yet it was only on challenging the new school that blame was apportioned to the old school for not sending the information through. What it amounts to in real terms, is that my child's 'specialist' educational needs have been sabotaged; In case of dyslexia, my understanding, is that such needs can be met in accord with policies and procedures -hence the question: Why is the school dragging its feet on matters to do with my child's educational needs? This has been happening since she was 9. Till now, there has been no steps in place to deal with the issues I am raising with the schools to conduct the right assessment; to date, the present school has performed their dyslexia screening, but refuse to do the full test.

SABOTAGE: POLICE CURRUPTION

On the 21 June 2012, I parked my car to pick up my child from Primary school in Bilborough. **"Lady you hit me"**, said a blonde-haired woman. *"Are you hurt?"* I asked **"No, but I suffer from kidney problem"** Two weeks later, Police dropped a note in my letter-box asking me to report to the station. On turning up I was told I'm being charged. *"Charged? What charge?"* For a start, no Officer was called to the scene of this supposed accident. What's more, no statement was taken from me. No crime number was issued.

How did Police get hold of my address details? Yet I was told in no uncertain terms that the matter was logged by the Crown Prosecution Service for a Court Hearing and the said woman is pressing for a £3,000 claim. My insurance company (Co-operative Insurance), came to my house, drew up documents and photographed my car for evidence and could find no marks whatsoever, subsequently coming to the conclusion that the whole thing was a fabrication.

An independent witness came forward to corroborate the woman's side of the story. The irony that brought an abrupt ending to this saga, resulted in a confession admitting that he was a friend of the woman. Her solicitor immediately pulled out; the witness in train, also pulled out thus making a travesty of the whole justice system, hence the question posed by my Solicitor: *How can a charge be brought against a defendant without any thorough investigation and evidence? However, things worked out in my favour because the case was dismissed.*

In the meantime, I firmly advised my Solicitor against dishing out any £3,000 claim on the pretext that this is FRAUD at the highest level. Here's a question for general members of the public to answer: would it not be a waste of tax payers' money if the Crown Prosecution Service proceeded to bring Court action where there's no evidence? How can the Police be believed when they have not even done their paperwork? This case is an eye-opener to levels of corruption that are endemic within the system; here's another question: is this case a one-off or are there other instances of mistrust among certain ranks of Officers within the force? A reader of this manuscript probably has a viewpoint on this.

- Chapter 32 -

MUM ABOUT TO BE CHUCKED OUT AFTER MORE THAN 40 YEARS

News came through a family member that my mum was taken to court by dad to get her off the property; this is a follow-on from divorce proceedings which had already been served on her.

If I am taking all of this as 'Gospel', I would like first of all to ask on what grounds is this divorced served? After the forty years of toiling day and night to cook, clean and raise nine children, **WHAT HAS SHE DONE TO DESERVE THIS?** In my estimation, something is wrong in the justice system in Jamaica. Given that eviction in practice will leave her homeless, invites yet another question: Where will she go?

According to the 1974 Matrimonial Act in the UK, women can actually issue divorce proceedings against their husbands if it can be proved that they have been subjected to a catalogue of domestic violence such as expressed in chapter 1 of this book. This new Act, at the instigation of Lord Denning, the then Master of the Rolls, was rushed through Parliament in order to allow married women experiencing severe brutality to say **ENOUGH IS ENOUGH!** Binding upon a settlement, such women can lay claim on percentages from the proceeds of their spouse be it from the estate or monies tied-up in banks.

Again I am posing the question: **WHAT CAN I UNDERSTAND FROM JAMAICA AND ITS JUSTICE SYSTEM, IF A MAN CAN BE ALLOWED TO BRUTALISE HIS WIFE YEAR IN YEAR OUT, ONLY TO THROW HER OUT OF THE HOUSE WITH NO FORM OF REDRESS OR RECOMPENSE?** This doesn't fit the criteria of a supposedly just society does it?

For a husband dedicated to church life and its values what is he saying to us? That it's all right to abuse women until they have reached an age when they can no longer undertake the rigours of house work any more? Where is the church in all of this? Should wives uphold values such as "wives be obedient to your husbands?" What about the one that says "husbands love your wives as Christ love the Church?

In the light of divorce proceedings that have already been served on my mum, it would be useful to seek legal advice with a view to re-opening the case and pressing for a settlement! **NEVER MUST IT BE SAID THAT HER EXCELLENT TRACK RECORD AS A TRUE AND FAITHFUL WIFE HAS BEEN OVER LOOKED!**

MOTHERHOOD

In terms of motherhood, it could also be argued that even if she thought of fighting for the rights of all nine of her children to get a good education, she would still be wasting her time trying to talk sense into my dad's head. He was far too domineering and dictatorial. As children, none of us could approach him on issues to do with our own advancement and that is sad! Finally, if it is true that he owns other houses, it could be argued that fear of the unknown albeit fear of death can drive men into making untimely decisions. i.e. turning mum out into outer darkness, is not going to solve the problem; what dad needs to do, is to come clean on a settlement with mum.

On my last visit after eleven years leaving Jamaica not seeing my dad for thirteen years , he was aware that my children and I were coming on holiday. On the phone, I asked if we could come and look for him. He coldly avoided the question until we returned back to the UK without seeing him. When I finally accosted him about this, he said **"IS COME YU COME FE TEK AWAY ME HOUSE -YOU AND YU MOTHER?"**

AFTERWORD

In conclusion all I'm trying to say through-out these chapters is; whatever you may go through look at the brighter side of life. If you don't give up God will turn your scars into stars. Even though my story may seem daunting and gloomy God knows what He was doing. He has the ability to divert storms but at times He will allow storms in our lives to push us into our destiny. May this book be an anchor and inspiration for those who are weak and for those who may need the extra strength to take them through challenging times.

To all Christians don't look at me as to ask why did I need to be so explicit. I had to because God wanted me to express my thoughts so others can identify with my story to bring healing. At times exposing a deed is the only way to defeat the enemy. Everyone is entitled to their opinions I dealt with these issues in order by writing this book in order to bring relief to me that my side of story can be heard.

Many times during my walk with God I have disobeyed and felt the consequences of bad choices. GOD GAVE EACH AND EVERYONE OF US A CONSCIENCE THAT GUIDES US.. THIS BOOK REFLECTS AN IMPERFECT CHRISTIAN WOMAN because of the Grace of God in my life has been spared to tell this story. God promised His strength will make us perfect in times of weaknesses.
Even though I have had some negative encounters with Christians please for all those who will read certain

chapters in this book try to understand that we are all human and there are no perfect Christians. We all have to give an account for the lives we live when Jesus return. These negative experiences I have had with some Christians is not the true reflection of Christianity. I continue to put my faith in God to take me through the rest of my journey because he is the one who has made me a SURVIVOR.

END